BEGINNER'S GUIDE TO GENEALOGY

FINDING YOUR FAMILY ROOTS

By

Janice Tuttle Friel

Completed 2018

This Book is dedicated to Muriel Sherlock who inspired me and for the courage of the millions of immigrants that were searching for a better future and In memory of my dear friend Cormac Kelly

BOOKS WRITTEN BY JANICE TUTTLE FRIEL

A DESCENDANT OF THE MAYFLOWER
THE HISTORY AND GENEALOGY OF THE
TUTTLE FAMILY

BRYAN'S ACRE
THE FRIELS OF DONEGAL

ACKNOWLEDGEMENTS

First and foremost I would like to thank my husband for encouraging me to write this book.

 I would also like to thank Ronald Rogers for his efforts in making this book a success with his hours of editing and his support and advice.

Heidi Nielsen who developed the cover for this book, I give special thanks for her hard work and excellent job.

To my daughter, Jeannine Friel for her skills and knowledge in editing documents/pictures within the book.

Thanks to all the people that helped in the completion of this book. I hope many will learn of their past and find their elusive ancestors to complete their story of their heritage.

THE STORYTELLERS

WE ARE THE CHOSEN. IN EACH FAMILY, THERE IS ONE WHO SEEMS CALLED TO FIND THE ANCESTORS. TO PUT FLESH ON THEIR BONES AND MAKE THEM LIVE AGAIN, TO TELL THE FAMILY STORY AND TO FEEL THAT SOMEHOW THEY KNOW AND APPROVE. DOING GENEALOGY IS NOT A COLD GATHERING OF FACTS, BUT INSTEAD, BREATHING LIFE INTO ALL WHO HAVE GONE BEFORE.

WE ARE THE STORYTELLERS OF THE TRIBE.

(AUTHOR UNKNOWN)

TABLE OF CONTENTS

CHAPTER I

GETTING STARTED

Are you obsessed with tracing your roots? You are not alone as thousands of people trace their family genealogy every day.

So why would you trace your roots? For me it was to discover where I came from… I had a family Bible with names and dates so who were these people? Where did they come from and how was I related to them. This became an adventure!

Genealogy isn't an easy task and you hit many road blocks along the way. It only takes that one discovery that gets those juices flowing to find out more. It's not that complicated if you know where to look. The computer will become your best friend. In this book I will show you where and how to look for "the roots of your life".

First, you want to collect all the information you can. Sit down with parents, grandparents, uncles, aunts, brothers and sisters. Make a list of questions you want to ask each person. Some of the information you receive from family members you will have to take with a grain of salt. Many times family stories are passed down from each generation and have no validity. You will have to document what they have told you. Tuck them in a folder and they may be of interest some day.

Organization is very important. Plan on putting each family member on a family chart and as you work down your tree you will be able to return to those charts.

The internet is a wonderful tool for research. This book will show you the websites for finding your roots. While some are paid sites, others are free so I will show you both avenues.

Make sure you document everything and make a hard copy when possible. Finding your family roots isn't just collecting names. You are building a story of your past generations and it should be factual.

Start your search with your grandparents. Where did they live? Where were they born, married and died. Search the state they resided in and the town. Many times you will find interesting facts about the area they lived in. Maybe it was a mining town and that your grandfather's occupation was a miner and after checking his death certificate you realized why he died of black lung.

Baby books, photo albums and scrapbooks are another great source for finding relatives. Many people have Family Bibles and recorded birth, marriage and death records in them. Look for family Bibles online as it seems they were established more in the 1800s and early 1900s. Here is a website for online Bibles. http://www.biblerecords.com/surnames.html

Do you have some old family photos but don't know what time period they are from? Well here are some tips in figuring that out. There are many clues in these photos and one is how they are dressed. In 1840 many women wore bonnets and 1900 men wore hats. Hair styles are another clue. Look for pictures online of people in the time frame you believe your ancestor was from. Look at their clothes and hair and even props used in the photo.

You never know what you will find along the way. In my case I traced my roots back to the Mayflower. When I started this quest I surely had no idea I would find myself looking at a relative on the famous ship. Not everyone will find someone famous but you may find some interesting facts along your journey.

Search each ancestor one at a time otherwise you will get overwhelmed. Sometimes you just need to take a break and then when you dive back into it you will have a fresh look.

Next step where do I find these documents? There are many sites available. Some are paid and some free. Start with the free ones. Make copies of all records.

Don't try to find all your ancestry in a week. Take your time and move slowly through each ancestor. You will need several documents to prove a certain item. Check birth, baptismal, death, marriage and census records or any other document you can obtain and check to see if they all have the same birth date. You will find discrepancies from one document to another. You will have to prove which one is right. By collecting several documents you then can prove which date is the correct one.

Make sure you complete all the information on one ancestor before moving on to the next. Too many times people will lose their focus and hit a brick wall and jump to the next ancestor. It's very important to try and complete one at a time. If you do hit a brick wall then move to someone within that family. Many times you will find additional information on a brother when searching another brother or sister or Aunt or Uncle.

When you have exhausted all possibilities in your research and cannot find anymore on you ancestry you can hire a professional genealogist. It will be less expensive if you give them all the information you have obtained yourself. You don't have to have them do your complete ancestry but maybe you only need help with one person. Make sure you find qualified people to do your research.

You can also subscribe to a paid genealogy website that may give you help. They usually are willing to sign you up for a yearly fee. What I have found is there are times when I don't have time in a certain month of the year so it could be a waste of money to subscribe for the full year. I have found out that you can subscribe for a month at a time. I like that as I can subscribe for the month I know I will have time to devote to genealogy and I can move from one paid website to another to get the maximum knowledge from all the sites. It's not one record that will tell you the story of your ancestor but many records.

One of the hardest things to find is a woman's maiden name. You can first try marriage and death certificates. When looking at census records there is a chance that one of the parents is either living in her home or living next door. Look at the whole census page before and after that page. You never know, there could be a family member living right down the street.

Sometimes you can figure out the maiden name through a child's name. Often a middle name of a child will be the surname of the parent and even a grandparent. On a death certificate there is usually an informant. An informant is the person who supplied the information to the funeral home so they could file the death certificate. Check out the last name of the informant as it could be that maiden name you were looking for. Also remember sometimes this information can be wrong depending on the relative. It could be a daughter-in-law who had limited information about the person. Even a direct family member would not know or forgot when someone was born or the deceased mother's maiden name.

Lastly check all children records including death records as the mother's maiden name may just be there. Pension records, Wills and burial records are another source in finding someone's maiden name.

Though this may be a place you will not want to find your ancestor you should also check prison and penitentiaries. A good website to look at which gives information by state would be

http://blacksheepancestors.com/

www.ancestorhunt.com/prison_search.htm

So if you can't find your ancestor in the census you should start looking in other places like prisons.

CHAPTER II

CENSUS RECORDS

Census records are a great place to start. There is a wealth of information. They began in the United States in 1790 and are available up to 1940. After 1940 they are not available due to the 72 year restriction. The 72 year rule is a waiting period by federal law that protects data for 72 years. Individual information will not be released for 72 years after it was collected. The last census that was released was the 1940 census which was released in 2012. The 1950 census will be released in the year 2022.

Keep in mind some records were destroyed during war time. The United States was the first country to conduct a regular census which is every ten years.

In many cases you can search not only by state but by county and township. For instance in the state of Delaware in the 1800 census you can search Kent, New Castle and Sussex counties and from those counties you can search by township.

You can access census records at the National Archives in Washington, DC or any of the regional locations. Here are the cities of the regional locations: Anchorage, Atlanta, Boston, Chicago, Denver, Ft Worth, Kansas City, New York City, Philadelphia, Riverside, San Francisco, and Seattle.

The US GenWeb project offers free census records access along with most public libraries and Daughters of the American Revolution (DAR) libraries. www.us-census.org

Another place to research census records is the Mormon website www.familysearch.org. Here you can search your ancestors name and it will not only bring up the census in the United States but other countries as well. Remember when searching for records make sure you use alterative spellings. The name BELL is a family name but I have also found it entered as BEALL and BEALE.

Online census free site:

http://www.census-online.com/links/

http://www.censusfinder.com/index.htm

In the 1790 US census, only the head of household and how many white male and female persons are listed according to age. The number of slaves owned is also listed.

In the 1800 – 1810 censuses, there are now 16 states for 1800 and 17 states in the 1810 census. What can be found in the censuses is head of household, white males and females according to age, other free persons, number of slaves, district or town and county.

Moving on to the 1820 census we have all of the above information and in addition we have the name of the slave owner, number of slaves, their ages, and the number of foreigners in the household. These people were not naturalized. There are 23 states included in the census now.

In the 1830 census we find all the above plus the number of deaf, dumb and blind persons in the household. There are now 24 states included in the census.

In the1840 census we have all of the above and now have included the age of the person receiving a military pension and persons attending school. We are now up to 26 states included in the census.

Don't give up on the pre 1850 census because you don't think there is much there. Try making a graph of all the census years with the name of your ancestor's age, the year and where that census (state) was taken. I have included a research checklist that has a census chart. It is located under Charts in Chapter XIV. Add any family members to that list that way you can track them easily. Pre 1850 census will show children and the age category they fit in and whether they are male or female. If you find children in later census you will know where they fit in the pre 1850 census.

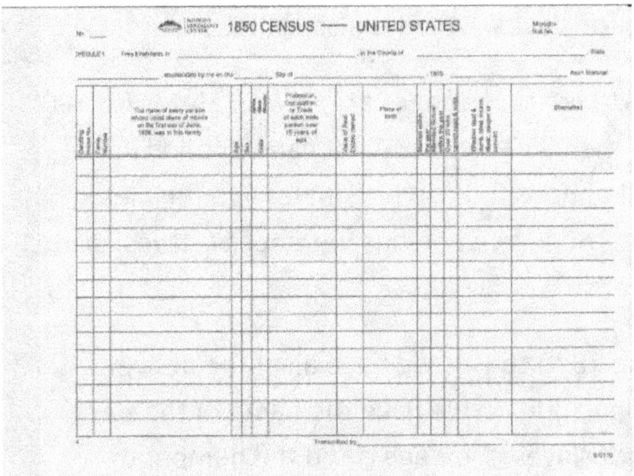
1850 CENSUS — UNITED STATES

In the 1850 - 1870 censuses all household members are listed but no relationship is added. This is the beginning of a much detailed accounting of who lived in the home.

We now have the name of the person, age, sex, race, birthplace, married within previous year, deaf, dumb, blind, occupation, education information, value of the home, and location. There are 31 states in 1850, 33 in 1860 and 37 in the 1870 census. In the 1870 census the value of personal estate has been added.

There is a slave schedule. There it lists the slave owner, age, gender and color of the slave. This is the first slave census that was taken separately from the regular census. There was also a mortality schedule in the 1850 census.

Another good source is the Mortality Schedule. This schedule gives you a list of people who died in the previous 12 months. The census lists the dead person's name, age, sex, race, married or widowed, birthplace, and month of their death, occupation and cause of death.

The 1880 census makes us feel like we hit the jackpot. We find all persons in the household, relationship to the head, age, sex, race, birthplace, marital status, marriage within previous year, month of marriage, deaf, dumb, blind, occupation, sick or disabled, each parents place of birth, education, value of real estate, street number, city, town and county.

So now we can figure out our relative's age, where he was born, if he was married and the month. It also gives us leads on where his parents were born. If they were born in another country it is one of the most valuable pieces of information. Now we know what country if any they immigrated from and can continue our search. We can even go to the house they lived in as we now have a street and number in the town and state.

Google earth is one way you can visit this address if you are not able to travel there. You simple put in the address and you are there. You can zoom down on the home and see exactly where they lived. The only down side of this depending on what year you are looking at and how many changes have occurred in that area. Your relative's home could now be a parking lot.

In 1890, we have a few items added to the census which gives us additional information that we can learn more about who our relatives were. They have added convicted prisoner, citizenship- years in US, naturalization, able to speak English, veterans- sailor or soldier during the Civil War.

In the 1900 census they have added the year they immigrated to the US. Now we have the ability to look for ship records as we will know the year they arrived. You have to be cautious with these dates as they may not be exactly but it gives you a good start. By the 1900 census 45 states are included.

MIDWEST GENEALOGY CENTER 1900 CENSUS —— UNITED STATES

Page No. ________

Supervisor's Dist. No. ________
Enumeration Dist. No. ________ Sheet No. ________

________ p or other division of County ________ , Name of Institution ________

Incorporated city, town, or village, within the above named division ________ Ward of City ________

Enumerated by me on the ________ day of June, 1900, ________ , Enumerator.

ON	NAME	PERSONAL DESCRIPTION										NATIVITY			CITIZEN			OCCUPATION	EDUCATION				HOME		
Family No.	of each person whose place of abode on June 1, 1900, was in this family	Relation to head of family	Color	Sex	Month of birth	Year of birth	Age at last birthday	Single, married, widowed, divorced	No. of years married	Mother of how many children	Number of these children living	Place of birth	Place of birth of father	Place of birth of mother	Year of immigration to U.S.	No. of years in U.S.	Naturalization	Occupation. Trade or Profession of each person ten years of age and over	No. of months not employed	Attended school (months)	Can read	Can write	Can speak English	Home owned or rented	Home owned free or mortgaged	Farm or house	Number of farm schedule

Transcribed by ________ Date ________

6-0070

As we move to the 1910 census we are again adding more pieces to the puzzle. Each person is named and the relationship is revealed to head of household. Here we will find children, Uncles and Aunts and if we are lucky sometimes the parents of the head of household. We can also find married children of the head of household and their wife's and their children names. Many times as a parent ages they move in with their children especially if one of the parents has passed away.

In the 1920 census there is additional information on the home, education, place of birth, native language, and occupation. We now have 48 states in the census. The 1930 census added what war the veteran served in.

The last census that is available is 1940. It appears to have much of what the 1910 and 1920 census has but they have added income/salary/wages.

If you go to the website: www.censusrecords.com you can print out a blank copy of any of the census years.

There were State censuses taken listed below. Keep in mind some of these censuses were destroyed.

Alabama 1818,1820,1821,1823, 1850,1855,1866,1907

Alaska 1870, 1878, 1879, 1881, 1885, 1887, 1890, 1895, 1904-1907, 1914, 1917

Arizona 1866, 1867, 1869, 1872, 1874, 1876, 1880, 1882

Arkansas 1823, 1829, 1865, 1911

California 1788, 1790, 1796, 1797, 1798, 1816, 1836, 1844, 1852

Colorado 1861, 1866, 1885

Delaware 1782

District of Columbia 1803, 1867, 1878

Florida 1825, 1855, 1866, 1867, 1868, 1875, 1885, 1895, 1913, 1945

Georgia 1798, 1800, 1810, 1827, 1834, 1838, 1845, 1852, 1853, 1859, 1865, 1879

Hawaii 1878. 1890, 1896

Indiana 1807, 1853, 1857, 1871, 1877, 1883, 1889, 1901, 1913, 1919, 1931

Iowa 1836, 1838, 1844, 1846, 1847, 1849, 1851, 1852, 1854, 1856, 1885, 1895, 1905, 1915, 1925

Kansas 1855, 1865, 1875, 1885, 1905, 1915, 1925

Louisiana 1853-1858

Maine 1837

Maryland 1776, 1778

Massachusetts 1855, 1865

Michigan 1837, 1845, 1854, 1864, 1874, 1884, 1888, 1894, 1904

Minnesota 1849, 1853, 1855, 1857, 1865, 1875, 1885, 1895, 1905

Mississippi 1801, 1805, 1808, 1810, 1816, 1818, 1820, 1822, 1823, 1824, 1825, 1830, 1833, 1837, 1840, 1841, 1845, 1850, 1853, 1860, 1866

Missouri 1797, 1803, 1819, 1840, 1844, 1852, 1856, 1860, 1864, 1876, 1880

Nebraska 1854, 1855, 1856, 1865, 1869 1885

Nevada 1862, 1863 1875

New Jersey 1855, 1865, 1875, 1885, 1895, 1905, 1915

New Mexico 1790, 1823, 1845, 1885

New York 1790, 1825, 1835, 1845, 1855, 1865, 1875, 1892, 1905, 1915, 1925

North Carolina 1780

North Dakota 1885, 1915, 1925

Oklahoma 1890, 1907

Oregon 1842, 1843, 1845, 1849, 1850, 1853, 1854, 1855, 1856, 1857, 1858, 1859, 1865, 1870, 1875, 1885, 1895, 1905

Rhode Island 1774, 1777, 1782, 1865, 1875, 1885, 1905, 1915, 1925, 1935

South Carolina 1825, 1839, 1869, 1875

South Dakota 1885, 1895, 1905, 1915, 1925, 1935, 1945

Tennessee 1891

Texas 1829-1836

Utah 1856

Virginia 1782, 1783, 1784, 1785, 1786

Washington 1856, 1857, 1858, 1860, 1871, 1874, 1877, 1878, 1789, 1880, 1881, 1883, 1885, 1887, 1889, 1891, 1892, 1898

Wisconsin 1836, 1838, 1842, 1846, 1847, 1855, 1865, 1875, 1885, 1895, 1905

Wyoming 1875-1878

Here is a list of states that had no census

Connecticut, Idaho, Illinois, Kentucky, Montana, New Hampshire, Ohio, Pennsylvania, Vermont, and West Virginia

Lastly when looking at a census record for an ancestor make sure you look at the page before and after as you never know if a family member is living down the street.

If you are in search of your Native American ancestors a good place to start is:

www.powwows.com/am-i-native

Why can't I find my ancestor in the census? There are several reasons this happens. They could have been in the hospital at the time or enlisted in the service during wartime and even in prison. Sometimes children were visiting a relative and were not there when the census taker arrived and the family for some reason never mentioned them. Children can also be gone from the home because they are now apprentice in another household. Husbands are missing due to their occupation and were not available or away on business. Maybe their name was written differently from census to census. They may have used their given name in the 1880 census and a nickname in the 1900 census. I have even seen names misspelled from census to census so poorly that you couldn't recognize they were the same person. The list goes on and on. Lastly census takers made mistakes for many reasons. They didn't know how to spell the name and didn't ask or if the person had a sharp accent the taker just didn't understand. There were mistakes surely made in census records so that is why you need multiple documents to prove a person's existence.

Ok so now we found our grandparents so how do we find their parents? The trick is finding the right parents! Many times I thought I had them and later through some document I found out I was wrong. It is very important to find the right document. Death records are probably the best source. Another source is the census and if you get lucky one of the parents just might be living with them. Newspapers can have birth announcements and social events of the family that would list parents. Of course there are Wills which lists children. If you know all your parents siblings and find a Will that list those siblings you know you have the right person.

There is one other way you can search your elusive ancestor. I logged on familysearch.org and entered my ancestor's first name, birth date, place of birth, residence and death date in the search area. What I received was several people with different surnames but one was my ancestor. The census taker had spelled the name Tittle instead of Tuttle.

CHAPTER III

BIRTH, MARRIAGE, DEATH AND DIVORCE

BIRTH

States didn't start keeping birth records until the early 1900s. Every state has their own start date for these records. If you are looking for a very early birth record it is usually held at a county level in that state. You may only find an index of births. An index of births is not an actual birth certificate but an abstract of the birth certificate. When searching these early birth records a good place to look is in historical societies. Some will hold them on microfilm and you will to go there to view them. Others will do a look-up usually for a fee.

While the 1900 census will show the birth month and year the 1850-1880 and 1910-1940 census will give the person's age. When searching for your relative first look in the 1850 census. After you locate him/her in the census you will see their age and place of birth. You can then subtract his age from the census year and come up with an approximate birth date. This will give you a good starting point to search for their birth record. You again can reach out to either a paid or free website. You can usually get to see an original copy of that relative's birth certificate. If you know the religion of your family member you can reach out to the church that could hold birth or baptismal records.

What are on these birth records? Here is what they usually include; a person's name, sex, race, place of birth, father's name, father's age, father's occupation, father's birthplace, mother's maiden name, mother's birthplace, number of children in the family and the date of the birth. Sometimes you will even see the family's resident address.

As you can see, there is a wealth of information and with the mother's maiden name, you can further your research.

Church records will usually show the name of the person born, name of parent, including mother's maiden name, date of birth, date of baptism, the Reverend's name and location of the church. If this record is from another country it can vary a little but most of the basic information is there, though in other countries it may not be written in English.

You can write or go to the Vital Statistics Office in the State where the birth occurred. There you can get a certified copy of the birth certificate. You will have to give the person's name, sex, parent names, month, day and year of the birth, place of birth, your connection to this person, and phone number.

Looking for records in New York? You can write to the address below.

New York Dept. of Health
Vital Records Section
Certification Unit
P.O. Box 2606
Albany, NY 12220-2602

The fee is $30.00 per copy of birth, marriage, death or divorce. The website is:

www.nyhealth.gov/vital_records/processingtime.htm

Many families kept a family Bible and noted birth records. Ask of the family if one exists. Of course you can also find these records on free and paid websites. If you know when your ancestor died you can go to:

http://www.searchforancestors.com/utility/birthday.html

Enter in the date and it will calculate the ancestor's birth year. This will give you an approximate birth date.

If you are trying to figure out someone's birth date and you have his death date maybe from his gravestone or death certificate then here is a good site to figure this out. Use the above website.

Here you enter the person's death date; day month and year and the age they were at death and this site will calculate their birth date.

Maps are another good source as they can display counties and towns around where your family lived. Many times they would move to an area closeby in maybe the next county or two towns over. If you have a map you can see these areas and check records for those areas for your ancestors.

Did your ancestor leave behind a yearbook from a school they attended? These too are good places to be looking. Check the school they went to and see if you can find a yearbook for that school. Many times students from a certain graduation class will have Facebook pages.

Another place to look for your ancestor records is service awards, pensions, and licenses for trades, job applications, unions, trade directories, wedding books, diaries, medical records, farm records, biographies, and all school records.

Now that you have found your immigrant ancestor, how do I find their birth date? Many times you will find the country of origin on a tombstone. Sometimes even family members will have these answers. Naturalization records are a place to find these. Maybe the father and mother were never naturalized, so what do I do now? Many times if you check one of the children's naturalization records it will give you the country of origin

You will need to find the town of origin. Once there, you can search the parish or civil records to then find birth records along with additional records.

Babies were baptized soon after they were born in the Catholic religion. A child who was illegitimate was still baptized in the church but it was up to the priest whether he was named in the document. If a family lived in a remote area births were not registered for weeks or even months after the birth.

Children who were abandoned when adopted were named by the church and in turn will give you clues to their origin in their name.

Certificate of Baptism

St. Patrick's Church
242 SOUTH 20TH STREET
PHILADELPHIA, PA

This is to Certify

That John Francis Friel

Child of William Friel

and Susan Wilson

born on the 14 day of Jany 1882 and

was Baptized

on the 29 day of January 1882

According to the Rite of the Roman Catholic Church

by the Rev. Thomas M. Power

the Sponsors being { Francis Crook
Mary Donohue

as appears from the Baptismal Register of this Church

Dated 9 Oct 1940

J. J. Valley
Pastor

JEFFERIES & MANZ, Phila.

Catholic Church Baptismal Record

State Birth Record

MARRIAGE

Marriage records can be difficult to find. You should first look for a church in the town that they lived before they were married. If you know their religion then search for the church closest to the bride's address.

When searching for a marriage record I usually take their birth year and add 18 to 21 years to that date. This is somewhat of a help in searching for that record. Also this is where the 1880 census records are so important there it lists marriage information. Other censuses that give us clues on marriage are 1850, 1860, and 1870. City directories are a place to look. It is a listing of salesmen and merchants who are adults living in a city. It lists name, address, occupation, and most important it lists the spouse's name.

At the Vital Statistics Office you can also get marriage records. To secure marriage records you will need the name of the bride and groom, day, month and year of marriage, relationship to the couple, and phone number.

Many times marriage records can be found in the newspapers. There is a paid website that offers a place to search for your relative and not only for marriages. You can also find death notices and birth announcements. You can find a tribute to a family member. When I was searching for my great grandfather in the newspapers I came across an article about the company he worked for. He had passed away and his company paid for the funeral and wrote a beautiful story about him. It also showed pictures of the place where he worked. This was a very special piece of material that I will keep forever.

Marriages in the 1700, 1800 and 1900s

Banns of marriage were announced in each person's church for 3 weeks on Sunday to let church members know that the couple was to marry. At this time anyone who objected to the marriage could voice their opinion.

"The purpose of banns is to enable anyone to raise any civil legal impediment to the marriage, so as to prevent marriages that are invalid. Impediments vary between legal jurisdictions, but would normally include a preexisting marriage that has neither dissolved nor annulled, a vow of celibacy, lack of consent, or the couples being related within the prohibited degrees of kinship."[1]

When applying for a marriage license they didn't have to wait the 3 weeks and could marry sooner. They first had to make an application and a pay sum of money which was a bond to make sure the information given was correct.

In a register office, marriage was by certificate and was by Banns. Also prior to 1837 you could not be married in a register office. A register office marriage is a civil marriage that is performed by an official and not by clergy.

Marriage bonds were sworn statements that there was no reason that the marriage should not take place. There was an amount of money that was paid and would be forfeited if the license wasn't complied with. The bond was sworn by one or more bondsmen to the church. The bondsmen were usually family members.

---

[1] Wikipedia, the free encyclopedia

Arranged marriages were an alliance between families. The two whom were to be wed had no say in the union. Today this practice is still used. Many times marriage was between first and second cousins.

Marriages dating back to the 1700s can sometimes be found in deed books and fee books. It wasn't unusual for a woman to marry at 15 or 16. Many marriages were what they called arranged marriages.

If someone married without their parent's approval they could be cut out of the will. Later in the 1800 and 1900s women would marry between 20 and 22. Most men in that timeframe would marry at age 26.

During the Civil War so many young men died and that didn't leave many choices for marriage, so they married older men and widowers. The age of consent in the 1800s was between 10 and 16.

Many times in Catholic marriage records you will find statements written by the officiating priest. It can include names of family members. Witnesses will also be named and can many times be family members. You can find these records on many paid sites or at churches or parishes through the country and even the world. In other countries some Catholic marriages can be written in Latin.

Anno 1924 die 12° mensis December Ego Josephus Sheridan
in Matrimonio conjunxi Joannem Hammond Donegal
filium Edvardi Hammond Donegal
et Margaritam Friel Beefpark Killymard
filiam Laurentii Friel " "
Præsentibus ⎤ Matthæo Martin Drumleigh
testibus ⎦ Catharina Gryffith Killymard

Here is the name of the groom in Latin which is Johnny Hammond. Filium means "son of" which is Johnny's father Edward Hammond. After "et" is bride Margaret Friel. Filiam means "Daughter of" which is Margaret's father Lawrence Friel. The witnesses are listed and it gives where all parties lived. This is an Irish Marriage record.

Here is a list of some English names and their counterparts in Latin

Albert- Albertus

Alfred- Alfredus

Alice- Alicia

Andrew- Andreas

Anthony- Antonius

Arthur- Arturus

Basil- Basilius

Frank- Franciscus

Beatrice- Beatrix

Bearnard- Bernardus

Charles- Carolus

Denis- Dionysius

Dorothy- Dorothea

Edward- Eduardus/Eduard

Ellen- Helena

Emily- Aemilia

Frances- Francesca

Helen- Helena

Henry- Henricus

Hugh- Hugo

Grace- Graye

James- Jacobus

Joan- Joanna

John- Joanne

Joseph- Josephus

Lawrence- Laurentius

Margaret- Margarita

Mark- Marcus

Mary- Maria

Matthew- Mattaeus

Maurice- Mauritius

Oliver- Olivarus

Patrick- Patricius

Philip- Philippus

Paul- Paulus

Ralph- Rudulfus

Richard- Richardus

Robert- Robertus

Stephen- Stephenus

Thomas- Thoma

Timothy- Timotheus

Walter- Gualteru

William- Guillelmus

Winifred- Winifrida

TUTTLE—BOWMAN—In Wellsburg, Jan 13th by
Rev Rufus Clark, Mr Oliver A Tuttle and Miss
Harriet E Bowman, all of Wellsburg.

CLARK—KILBURN—Monday evening, Jan 21st,
at the house of Ezra Clark, Orley S Clark and
Miss Jennie L Kilburn.

DIED.

JONES—In Tryonville, Jan'y 20. Alexander
Jones, aged about 55 years.

GABLE—In Mead tp, January 24, Ambrosia,
daughter of Thomas and Tabitha Gable, aged
15 years.

LARIMER—In Conneautville, January 23d, of
consumption, Joseph Larimer, aged 45 years
and 17 days.

SMITH—In Spring, Jan 17th, of paralysis of the
heart, Almon Smith, aged 74 years, 1 month
and 6 days.

MARSH—In Spring tp, Jan 18th, of obstruction
of the bowels, Hiram, son of Jerome Marsh,
aged 19 years.

HARPER—In Summit tp, Jan 10th, Rob't Harper, aged 80 years and 8 months.

WILLIAMSON—In South Shenango, Jan 10th,
John Williamson, in the 87th year of his age.

SMITH—In Lockport, Erie county, Jan 11th of
asthma, George R Smith, in the 78th year of

Example of a marriage announcement in the newspaper

You can find local history in the town they lived in. Maybe the town was hit with the plague or there was a terrible train crash. You never know where it will lead you and what you may find.

If your family member lived in a city then City Directories is a great place to find a spouse and her name. There you find the person's name, address and occupation. Wives are usually listed as well.

This Certifies That

Elvene E. Tuttle

of Leestershire New York

and

Elsie R. Showalter

of Leestershire New York

Were by me united in the bands of

Holy Matrimony

According to the ordinance of God, and the Laws of the

State of New York

On the Nineteenth day of March

In the year of our Lord one thousand nine hundred and Thirteen

At Leestershire New York

Minister of the Gospel

Witnessed by

Beatrice E. Cole, Miss Tuttle

Marriage record found in a family Bible

State marriage record

DEATH

Death records can be found in several places. In a census record if the spouse is absent from the record this is a good indication the person has passed. You must be careful because there are other reasons that a person could be absent from the record. One could be that the couple is divorced or the husband had joined the service. Checking the age of the relative in the previous census record can indicate that he was up in years and probably did die. Then you can start looking for a death certificate around the year of the census.

Start looking for deaths in journals, diaries, family Bibles, and military records. Lastly from the years 1850 to 1880 census show people who died in the Mortality Schedules. In the city directories if the husband is deceased he will still be listed along with his wife but she will be listed as widow.

Some countries have their own newspaper and list obituaries. You would need to know what country your ancestor once lived but it can pay off. Here is an example of what you could find.

The Irish American newspaper listed obituaries of people who died in the US but were originally from Ireland. In the obituaries it will list the person's name, date of death, townland and county in Ireland he/she was from, sometimes lists the family members, funeral home, date and time of funeral in the US. You can find these newspapers at Genealogybank.com and other paid sites. You can also find listings of marriages, births, and passenger lists in these newspapers.

You need to find out if a death record exists for that state and year. For example the State of Pennsylvania death records are available from 1906-1964. You can get death records from the Clerk of Orphans Court at each county courthouse from 1893-1906. If they passed away in the mid to late 1800s the mortality schedule may be of some help.

1850 AND 1860 FEDERAL MORTALITY SCHEDULES

Ending-   State-   County-   Town/Township-

| Name of every person who died during the year ending the 1st of (1850 or 1860), whose usual place of abode at time of death was in this family. | Description | | | Free or Slave | Married or widowed | Place of Birth (Naming the State, Territory, or Country) | The month in which the person died | Profession, Occupation, or Trade | Disease or cause of death | Number of days ill |
	Age	Sex	Color (Black, White, Mulatto)							
1	2	3	4	5	6	7	8	9	10	11

aka:

National Archives and Records Administration   NARA's website is www.archives.gov   NA Form 14131a (3/05)

Again these records can be found in free and paid websites. If they are early death years then you can check with the area historical society and see if they have a record. You can write to the Vital Statistics Office in the state the death occurred and get a certified copy or a genealogical copy.

Social Security Death Index is another place you can find deaths. These records are available from 1962 forward. You can search these records by entering the person's name at:

https://www.familysearch.org/search/collection/1202535

What you will find on the record is the name of the deceased, age, birth date, last residence and death date.

Obituaries in newspapers are another good source if you know the state where that person died. Look for the local newspaper in the town they lived in for obituaries.

Many times you can find death dates along with other information on your ancestor at the Elk's, Mason's, Women's club and Red Cross.

Did your relative work for the Railroad? The National Archives has information about Retirement Board Records. https://www.archives.gov/atlanta/public/railroad-retirement-board-records

Ancestry.com a paid site also has records on the Western Railroad Employment Records from 1935-1970.

The Death Index website gives you deaths by State. www.deathindexes.com/

Fallen Police Officers- You can search by state and name

http://www.odmp.org/search/browse

Old Virginia Obituaries- Search by surname from 1790-1940

http://virginiaobits.homestead.com/

Legacy.com- has 200 million obituaries.

www.legacy.com

At Findagrave.com you can find burials which will many times give you a place to look for your deceased relative. This is the world's largest gravesite collection. You can search by name, year of birth, year of death or cemetery. If you are not sure where they are buried first search by name. If that doesn't turn anything up then search by the state you know your relative lived in when they died. Once you find your ancestor here is what you will find in the cemetery record. Name, birth, death, name of cemetery where the burial took place, a plot location, and sometimes there will be a picture of the gravestone. Many times they will also show the spouse or other family members if they are buried in the same cemetery. You can also find listed on the burial site additional information that other family members have added like military record, along with pictures of the deceased person.

You will need to set up an account but it is free.

www.findagrave.com

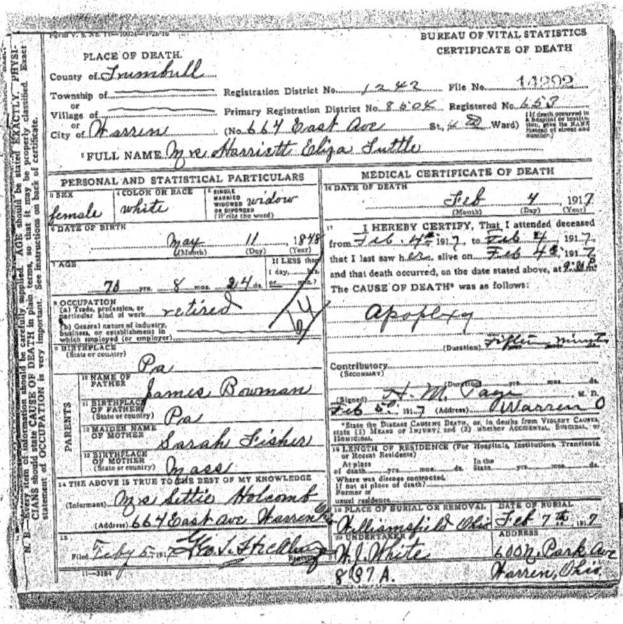

BUREAU OF VITAL STATISTICS
CERTIFICATE OF DEATH

PLACE OF DEATH.
County of Trumbull
Township of .... Registration District No. 1242 File No. 14292
or Village of .... Primary Registration District No. 8608 Registered No. 658
or City of Warren (No. 664 East Ave St., 2 Ward)
FULL NAME Mrs. Harriett Eliza Tuttle

PERSONAL AND STATISTICAL PARTICULARS
SEX female. COLOR OR RACE white. SINGLE, MARRIED, WIDOWED OR DIVORCED widow
DATE OF BIRTH May 11 1848 (Month) (Day) (Year)
AGE 78 yrs. 8 mos. 24 ds.
OCCUPATION (a) Trade, profession, or particular kind of work retired
(b) General nature of industry, business, or establishment in which employed (or employer)
BIRTHPLACE (State or country) Pa.
PARENTS
NAME OF FATHER James Bowman
BIRTHPLACE OF FATHER (State or country) Pa.
MAIDEN NAME OF MOTHER Sarah Fisher
BIRTHPLACE OF MOTHER (State or country) Mass.
THE ABOVE IS TRUE TO THE BEST OF MY KNOWLEDGE
(Informant) Mrs. Lettie Holcomb
(Address) 664 East Ave Warren O.
Filed Feby 5 1917 Geo. V. Shelling Registrar

MEDICAL CERTIFICATE OF DEATH
DATE OF DEATH Feb 4 1917 (Month) (Day) (Year)
I HEREBY CERTIFY, That I attended deceased from Feb 4th 1917, to Feb 4, 1917, that I last saw her alive on Feb 4th 1917, and that death occurred, on the date stated above, at 9.30 P.M.
The CAUSE OF DEATH was as follows:
apoplexy
(Duration) fifteen minutes
Contributory (Secondary)
(Signed) H. M. Page M.D.
Feb 5th 1917 (Address) Warren O
LENGTH OF RESIDENCE (For Hospitals, Institutions, Transients or Recent Residents)
PLACE OF BURIAL OR REMOVAL Williamsfield Ohio DATE OF BURIAL Feb 7th 1917
UNDERTAKER H. J. White ADDRESS 600 N. Park Ave Warren, Ohio
8197 A.

N. B.—Every item of information should be carefully supplied. AGE should be stated EXACTLY. PHYSICIANS should state CAUSE OF DEATH in plain terms, so that it may be properly classified. Exact statement of OCCUPATION is very important. See instructions on back of certificate.

Example of a death certificate

Here it shows the person's name and parent's name, where James Bowman was born, Pa. and Sarah Fisher born Pa. giving us her maiden name.

Sometimes we find our ancestor's death record but are disappointed because we can't read it all for one reason or another. It may be important to you to know the cause of death and if so, we have a way to find it. This code was available from 1898 forward. There are many countries that use this code. It can be found on documents from your ancestors in their country of origin. The database is updated every 10 years.

There is a number on death certificates that people have no idea what that it is. (See death certificate on page 37) The number on the certificate is from ICD (International Classification of Disease). If you look at the death record above you will see the number 64 circled and hand written in the middle of the record. You can look up this number and find the cause of death. This information is available on Wolfbane Cybernetic online. http://www.wolfbane.com/icd/index.html

Our relative has the number 64 and she died in 1917. We would go to Revision 2 (1909). There by clicking on the revision and paging down to 64A we see that she died of apoplexy which in our case is exactly what is on her death certificate. If it had not been there we would not know what she died from.

The revisions are set up by years. Revision 1 is 1900, 2-1909, 3-1920, 4-1929, 5-1938, 6-1948, 7- 1955, 8-1965, 9-1975 and 10-1990. You should always choose the revision date before your ancestor's death date.

Here are some medical conditions and their meaning

Cholera-   acute infection of the bowel

Diphtheria- a contagious disease of the throat. Similar to scarlet fever

Typhoid Fever- a water borne illness from unsanitary conditions. It is also called Bilious fever, ship fever & spotted fever

Malaria- Transmitted by mosquitoes. Chill fever

Consumption- Tuberculosis

Bright's disease- Kidney failure

Apoplexy- Stroke or cerebral hemorrhage

Pox- Small Pox

American Plague- Yellow fever

Dysentery- inflammation of the colon

Lung Fever- Pneumonia

Quinsy- tonsillitis

DIVORCE

To find this record you will first have to have the name of both persons, date of divorce, county and state it took place. If you know the county and state the divorce occurred in then you can write or call the county's Clerk of Courts Office and request a certified copy. If you don't know the county it happened in then contact the Department of Vital Records in the state it took place. Try and pin down a date to search for their divorce if you do not know the exact date. First try the census and see when the wife is missing. One important thing is to know the laws of the times.

Many times historical societies will have these records and could date back 100 years, though divorce was not as common as it is today. In divorce records you can find how long a couple was married and how many children they had and where they lived.

Newspapers are another source for these records and some Civil War records will list wives and children from other marriages.

www.google.com is a great place to find out the particular laws in the year and state your ancestor lived to learn more about their divorce.

One thing you find out in earlier years is that in a divorce if any land was owned by the wife prior to her marriage became property of the husband.

Divorce records are mostly public records, but in some cases they are sealed. It is usually done due to private information that isn't to be made public. Divorce can also be found in the 1900 census records where they ask if you are single, married, widowed or divorced.

What you will find on a divorce record is the husband and the wife's names, marriage date, property, child custody and marriage place. It may describe facts about the husband or wife and why they are asking for this divorce.

Sometimes you can find scandalous things within the family. This is another way you will start to see the whole character of your ancestor. You must look at the customs of the times. What may be unheard of today was common in the 1700s.

So many times women married at a very young age to older men. Even men would abandon their wives due to debt and the wife would file for divorce. This was to protect her from his debtors.

Also a husband may divorce his wife because she was infertile and then marry another. In the Hebrew religion if his brother died he was required to marry the widow.

CHAPTER IV

MILITARY RECORDS

Military records begin with the Revolutionary War through to the Vietnam War. Information for draft records is available for the Civil War, WWI and WWII. Pension records are available for the Revolutionary War, War of 1812, and the Civil War. Civil War draft records are found at the National Archives and regional locations around the country.

First step you must find what war your ancestor fought in if any. Depending on the war your ancestor fought in there could be a great source of information in these records.

So where do I find out if my ancestor was in a war. Here are the places to look. Obituaries, historians, cemeteries/tombstones, 1890 Civil War Veterans census, pension indexes, (available through Ancestry and Family search). Organization Index to Pension files of Veterans (available through 3Fold).

www.ancestry.com

www.familysearch.com

www.3fold.com

Look for ancestors in family photos who may be wearing a uniform or newspaper clippings that were saved.

A person did not have to be a citizen to serve in the military and you still don't to this day, though it is encouraged.

The Rangers served in the 1600s and 1700s in the war between the colonists and Indians. They were full time soldiers, scouts and guides. Next there was the Militia which was created by local governments. They were mostly all white free men. This militia system was used by the thirteen colonies. They usually served about 6 to 8 months.

Many women were involved in the Civil War and went with their husbands. They did women's work like laundry, cooking and nursing. During the Civil War many worked in hospitals.

This tombstone of my ancestor shows he was a part of the GAR which is the Grand Army of the Republic. It is a fraternal organization of veterans who served in the Civil War. With this information from the tombstone I was able to search and receive his Civil War pension records.

After I found the regiment of my relative I was able to find what it was like during those times. He belonged to the 137th regiment organized out of Binghamton, NY on 9/25/1862. With that information I was able to look at the history of that regiment. It told me of the battles they fought, list of causalities, muster roll and unit roster. Now I was getting a real image of the life my great great grandfather lived.

Registration records offer birth date, marriage and even naturalization records. It will also give you address, occupation, height and color of hair and eyes.

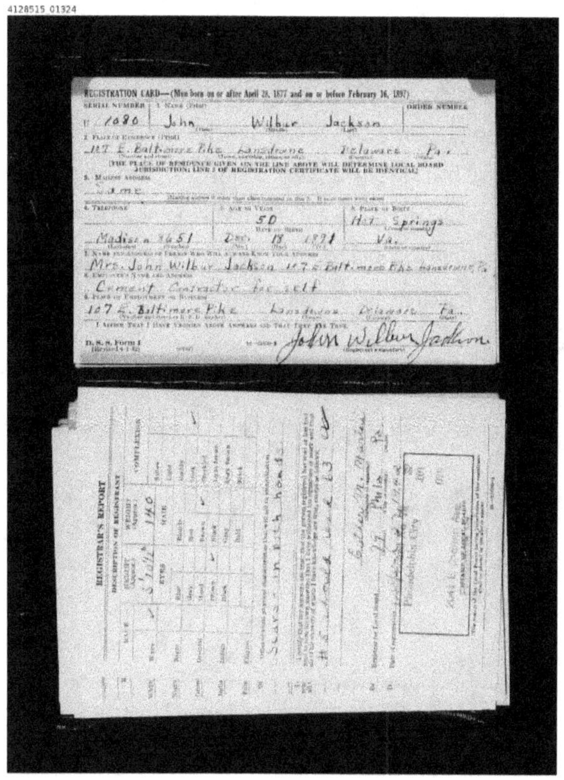

Civil War Union registrations give you, age, race, occupation, marital status, state or country born. People who were exempt from serving were people who were physically or mentally unable, only son to a widowed parent, widower with children and convicted felon.

Civil War Confederate required all white males to register between the ages of 18 to 35 years old but by 1864 the age jumped 17 to 50.

People who were exempt from the Civil War were ministers, teachers, civil officials, tradesman, railroad employees and plantation owners. You could also hire someone to take your place in the war if you paid a large sum of money.

World War I draft began in 1917 and the draft board was created. Men between 18 and 45 were required to register. Some of the questions that were asked when registering were name, age, address, birth date, occupation, birth place, citizenship status, employer, race, height, color of hair and eyes. You can find these records on paid and free sites like familysearch.org.

WWI Draft Registration
Card A issued for June 5, 1917

The WWI Draft Registration Reference Report can be used in conjunction with this data sheet.

| Form 1 | **REGISTRATION CARD** | No. _______ |

1 Name in Full _______________________________ Age in Years
(Given Name)   (Family Name)

2 Home Address _______________________________
(No.)   (Street)   (City)   (State)

3 Date of Birth _______________________________
(Month)   (Day)   (Year)

4 Are you (1) a natural-born citizen, (2) a naturalized citizen, (3) an alien, (4) or have you declared your intention (specify which)? _______________________________

5 Where were you born? _______________________________
(Town)   (State)   (Nation)

6 If not a citizen, of what nation are you a citizen or subject? _______________________________

7 What is you present trade, occupation, or office? _______________________________

8 By whom employed? _______________________________
Where employed? _______________________________

9 Have you a father, mother, wife, child under 12, or a sister or brother under 12, solely dependent on you for support (Specify which)? _______________________________

10 Married or single (Which)? _____________ Race (Specify which)? _____________

11 What military service have you had? Rank _____________ Branch _____________
Years _____________ Nation or State _____________

12 Do you claim exemption from draft (Specify grounds)? _______________________________

I affirm that I have verified above answers and that they are true.

____
(Signature or Mark)

If person is of African descent cut off this corner.

REGISTRATRAR'S REPORT

1	Tall, medium, or Short (Specify which)? _________ Slender, medium, or stout (Which)? _________
2	Color of eyes _________ Color of hair _________ Bald _________
3	Has person lost foot, arm, leg, hand, eye, or both Eyes or is he otherwise disabled (Specify)? _________

I certify that my answers are true, that the person registered has read his own answers, that I have witnessed his signature, and that all of his answers of which I have knowledge are true, except as follows

____

(Signature of Registrar)

Precinct _________

City or County _________

State _________

(Date of Registration)

National Archives and Records Administration   NARA's website is www.archives.gov   NA Form 14133a (4/05)

WWII draft was still in existence in 1920 to 1930s. Because of the bombing at Pearl Harbor in 1941 many men volunteered to serve. Some of the questions that were asked which will give you information you may be looking for were name, age, birth date, birthplace, address, phone number, contact person, their address, race and physical appearance. These original records for both wars can be found at the National Archives.

The 1930 census will show any military war your ancestor may have been in and will show if they were a Civil War veteran.

The National Archives is a great place to start as they have compiled service records, pension applications and pension payment records. You can find these records on the Fold3 website.

Bounty Land Warrant applications are files between 1775 and 1855. This would include the Revolutionary War, War of 1812, Indian Wars and Mexican war. It holds documents much like pension files. There are several places you can find these records other than the National Archives. For a fee you can find them at Fold3.com and Ancestry.com

You can search for a burial place of your veteran at National Cemetery Administration. https://gravelocator.cem.va.gov/

Let's start with the Revolutionary War. Of course the most common place to find these records is on paid websites. Many of these records were destroyed. National Archives have many of these records on microfilm and can be viewed at their locations. There are also many printed books on the Revolutionary War where you can find additional information.

http://www.militaryindexes.com/revolutionarywar/

The above website is an excellent place to learn about this war. There you will also find information for the War of 1812, Mexican War, Civil War, WWI, WWII, Korean War and Vietnam War.

Fold 3 is a good paid site to look for your military ancestors where you can search by name and state. The National Archives in Washington, DC and regional centers. For records of WWI

and to the present you should contact National Military
Personnel Records Center in St. Louis, Missouri.

War of 1812 records at the National Archives gives you Pension
and Bounty Land Warrant Application files and military service
records.

 Union and Confederate pension records are available at the
National Archives in Washington, DC and online. If you want a
paper copy you will need to use NATF form 86 for each soldier.
You can get this at www.achives.gov search forms. You can also
write to National Archives and Records Administration, Attn.
NWCTB, 700 Pennsylvania Ave. NW, Washington, DC 20408-
0001.

I requested my Great-grandfather's pension records and
received 106 pages of records. In it there was the name of his
wife and children with some birth dates and the state where
they were born. Also to my surprise a second wife and several
addition children by this wife with birth dates. This record gave
me an innumerous amount of information. It gave birth and
health records. Before I received these records I had no idea
where he was born.

Pension records are based on service in the armed forces in the
United States between 1775 and 1916. You can find anything
from birth certificates, death certificates, and marriage
certificates to family Bibles.

Draft records are another great source. Remember there was
no draft after 1973. There you will find name, residence, birth,
physical description, occupation and marital status.

Bounty land warrant application files are from wars served between 1775 and 1855. If your ancestors were in the Revolutionary War, War of 1812 or the Mexican War these records can hold genealogical information. They were granted land for serving.

WWI draft registration cards will give you basic information. It also holds African American records.

WWII records can be searched
https://aad.archives.gov/aad/index.jsp

For the Vietnam War information you will have to request form SF-180 to get records from National Archives.

Civil War Manuscript Collection-
http://spec.lib.vt.edu/civwar/guidecw.htm

Soldiers and Sailors of the Civil War

https://www.nps.gov/civilwar/soldiers-and-sailors-database.htm

PA State Archives Civil War Veterans Card File 1861-1866
https://www.nps.gov/civilwar/soldiers-and-sailors-database.htm

Looking for Military prisoner records?

www.genealogytoday.com/sitemap.html

Pennsylvania State Archives

Civil War Veteran Card File 1861-1866 Indexes-
http://www.digitalarchives.state.pa.us/archive.asp

Mexican Border Campaign Veteran Card File Indexes-
http://www.digitalarchives.state.pa.us/archive.asp?view=Archiv
eIndexes&ArchiveID=9

WW I Service Medal Application Cards Indexes-
http://www.digitalarchives.state.pa.us/archive.asp?view=Archiv
eIndexes&ArchiveID=6

**Spanish American War Veterans Card File of United States
Volunteers**

http://www.digitalarchives.state.pa.us/archive.asp?view=Archiv
eIndexes&ArchiveID=8

 Revolutionary War Military Abstract Card File Indexes-
http://www.digitalarchives.state.pa.us/archive.asp?view=Archiv
eIndexes&ArchiveID=13

Militia Officers Index Cards 1775-1800

http://www.digitalarchives.state.pa.us/archive.asp?view=Archiv
eIndexes&ArchiveID=18

 PA National Guard Veterans Card File 1867-1921

http://www.digitalarchives.state.pa.us/archive.asp?view=Archiv
eIndexes&ArchiveID=21

CHAPTER V

IMMIGRATION, NATURALIZATION & SHIP'S LISTS

Immigration started in this country in the 1600s on the east coast. Jamestown, Virginia was one of those settlements. Many left their homelands due to religious persecution, famine and a strong desire to secure a better life.

The government required all captains of a ship arriving from another country to supply a passenger list starting in 1820.

What exactly is on an immigration record? You will find their birthplace, ship name, age, height, eye and hair color, occupation, last residence, name and address of where they are going, and the amount of money in their possession.

The records will be listed by Port of Arrival. The main ports were New York, Boston, Baltimore, Philadelphia and New Orleans. There were also smaller ports that are listed by state at this website below.

www.genesearch.com/ports.html

You can order passenger lists from 1800-1959 at the National Archives online: you will need form 81.

You will need to know the port of arrival by your ancestor if you are looking for passenger lists in the US. Most all passenger lists were written by hand and sometimes difficult to read. Make sure you keep in mind the spelling on the surname as it could be different than it is spelled today.

If your ancestor settled along the Mississippi River then look at New Orleans or Galveston, Texas. Maybe your family lived in Philadelphia or Pittsburgh, Pa. then I would be looking at Philadelphia or Baltimore port of arrival. Living along the Ohio River I would look at Philadelphia or Baltimore ports.

Passenger lists located at the New York port of arrival would be of interest to those searching New York, northern Pennsylvania and Canada. When looking for passenger lists for all of the New England States you would find them at the Boston port of arrival.

Many of your ancestors fled their homelands due to many factors. Look for events in their countries that would drive them out to find shelter in places like America. You can find passenger lists exiting those countries.

New Orleans, Louisiana was an immigration port. You can search these records at
http://www.genesearch.com/neworleans/quickguide.html

Passengers arriving at this port came from the West Indies, Spain, Germany, and France. Slaves from the Caribbean arrived at this port, also. In the 1880s the Irish were the largest group of immigrants that landed in the port of New Orleans.

 Liverpool, England was the most popular port in Europe to America in the 1800s. They immigrated and became farmers or were involved in agriculture. Many also came because they had a skill that was useful in America. Some of those skills were textiles, stonemasons, shopkeepers, tailors and saloon owners.

In 1850, over 960,000 people immigrated to the US from Ireland. By 1854 a quarter of the population in the US immigrated in a 10 year period. New York State welcomed German immigrates while the French made their homes in New York, Chicago, New Orleans and Quebec, Canada.

The Italians didn't come until after 1870. They left Italy due to high taxes and low wages and were mostly men. From 1790 to 1849 people immigrated to the US because of inexpensive farmland. They came from Britain, Ireland, and Germany. When the Irish came they were responsible for building many of our railroads and worked in textile factories and mills.

Five million Germans immigrated between 1850 and 1930

Many people immigrated to Australia not by choice but because they were convicted of a crime by the British government. They were convicted of simple crimes and some more serious crimes.

Virginia along with other southern states brought slaves into the country from Africa and Ireland. The Irish were known as white slaves.

The first place I would look would be the census record. There it will give you in the 1850-1940 censuses the country of birth. In the 1900-1930 censuses it will give you the year your ancestor immigrated. You can then search for a passenger list or ship's records.

Here is a good place to search ship and passenger lists from different countries. http://khuish.tripod.com/ships.htm. Here it will give you the name of the ship, date it departed and the destination. The passenger list will give you the person's name, age, people travelling with them and their names and ages, and their sex. This site will also give you other great sites for ship's lists.

In the 1870 census it will tell you if the parents were foreign born and in the 1880-1930 census it will give you the parent's birthplace. Once you have this information you then search the country they originated from.

Death certificates are another place you could find where a relative was born. It will sometimes tell you where the parents were from. You should take a look at the death certificate in Chapter Three "Birth, Marriage, Death and Divorce".

Through Familysearch.com you can search Index to Bounty Immigration. In these records you will find persons on immigrant ships from 1823-1842 to Australia and New South Wales. This site makes available many free searches from passenger lists to individual country lists. When searching go to familysearch.org, then at the top of the page click search, then page down to the bottom of the page and you will see "Find a Collection" in the space provided type in immigration. There it will bring up all the sites available to you on immigration. In addition you can also look in the 1930 census where you will find the year immigrated to the US.

If in the 1870 census you find a check mark under "male citizens of US of 21 yrs of age and upward," this means they were naturalized by 1870. In the 1900-1930 censuses you can find if a person was naturalized. The naturalization records can be found at the National Archives, Federal court or County court.

Of course the National Archives is a place to go to find immigration records. There will also be ship passenger arrival records and on these you will find place of birth, the name of the ship and date of entry, age, height, eye and hair color, occupation and last residences. These records are available from 1820-1982 and you will have to search at the port of arrival.

Here are some websites you can search for ancestors.

The National Archives website

https://www.archives.gov/research/immigration/passenger-arrival.html

Immigration Passengers Arrival

https://aad.archives.gov/aad/series-list.jsp?cat=GP44

Where you can search passengers coming in from other countries

Ellis Island

www.libertyellisfoundation.org

What you will find at Ellis Island is passenger lists and immigration records from 1820-1957 who arrived at the port of New York. It holds individuals that also arrived at Castle Garden from 1855-1890 and the Barge Office from 1890-1892. Over 12 million immigrants passed through there. When researching on Ellis Island you will find a ship name and list of passengers. Make sure you look at the entire page of passengers because there could be other family members listed on another page or further down the page.

Ships list 1847

http://www.theshipslist.com/1847/index.htm

There were 29 questions that were asked of the immigrants when they came through Ellis Island. Name, age, sex, married or single, occupation, able to read or write, neutrality/country, race, last residence, name and address of relative in native country, final destination, do they have a ticket to their final destination, who paid their passage, do they have $50, were they ever in the US before, if joining up with relative give name and address, ever in prison, whether a Polygamist, whether a Anarchist, are they coming with any promise or agreement of labor, condition of health, crippled, height, complexion, race eyes and hair, identifying marks and place of birth.

So as you can see there is a wealth of information.

SHIPS LISTS

http://www.immigrantships.net/

 There is a search block where you can search for ancestor or ship

Film Publication Number: ________

Number: ________

Group: ________

List: ________

Customs List of Passengers

| August 1882 to March 1903 |

+   To be used for all passengers
++ To be used for cabin passengers only
*   To be used for passengers other than cabin passengers

the City of New York

w York

I, ________ Master of the ________ do solemnly, sincerely and truly swear that the following List or Manifest subscribed by me, and now delivered by me to the Collector of the District of the City of New York, is a full and perfect list of all the passengers taken on board said vessel at ________ from which port or ports the said vessel has now arrived; and that on said list is truly the age, sex, calling or occupation, the port of embarkation, the number of pieces of baggage of all passengers as to a protracted sojourn in this country, and also, in regard to Cabin passengers, the country of which they are and of passengers other than cabin passengers, their native country, their intended destination or location in the United States, and whether they are citizens of the United States, or not, and the location of the compartment or space y each, as required by the Passenger Act of 1882 and the Regulations of the Secretary of the Treasury. So help me God.

Sworn to before me this ________ day of ________ 18____

________ Deputy Collector   ________ Master

2 +	3 +		4 +	5 +	6 ++	7 *	8 *	9 *	10 +	11 *	12 +	13 +	14 +
Name in Full	Age		Sex	Calling or occupation	Country of which they are citizens	Native Country	Intended destination or location, State, or Territory	State of passengers other than Cabin, whether Citizens of the United States	Transient, in transit, or intending protracted sojourn	Location of compartment or space occupied forward, amidships or aft	Number of pieces of baggage	Port of embarkation	Date and cause of death
	Yrs.	Mos.											

National Archives and Records Administration   NARA's website is www.archives.gov   NA Form 14132b (3/03)

Other places to look are Canadian border crossing records, and Mexican border crossing records, Chinese immigration records, Italian immigration records entering US, Irish Famine passenger records, passport applications, crew lists, customs records, deportation, register of seamen and many more. All available at the National Archives online Archival database. (AAD)

One unexpected place to find immigration records is newspapers. They sometimes posted immigrant arrivals in the paper. In Wiki you will find Passengers, indentured servants, apprentices and estate probates.

Remember when checking passengers lists your ancestor could have traveled back and forth to his homeland to visit family but was now a US citizen so his/her place of origin would be the US.

Naturalization

It is a process for a person over the age of 18 to obtain citizenship. In the 1920 census it will show the year the person was naturalized. The process begins with declaring your intent to be naturalized. After two or three years you submit a petition to become a citizen and after it is approved you become a citizen.

During colonial times British immigrants were automatic citizens. After the Revolutionary War naturalization was set up by each state. Immigrants could be naturalized in any court that performed naturalization. This could be city, county, state or federal court. In 1906 it was performed mostly in federal courts. Check the courts where your ancestors lived for their naturalization records first. You will not find country of origin on these records until after 1906. One thing you probably will not find in these records is names of parents.

Citizenship

A Citizenship certificate is issued to an individual who was born outside the US. Citizenship is granted by birth or through naturalization. You are not required to apply for citizenship.

To better understand this, here is an explanation. Let's say your parents come to the US from another country and leave you back in the homeland. Later they decide to bring you to the US. You are already a citizen by birth even though your birth certificate states you were born in another country. If you are 18 years old or under you automatically become a US citizen. In the 1930 census it will give citizenship status. Immigrant children under age 16 received their citizenship through their parents.

Summary: Citizenship is granted to people who are born to parents who are already citizens of the country. Naturalization is granted to people who are citizens of another country.

Declaration of Intention

This is a document filed in court for someone who intends to become a US Citizen. It is the beginning of the Naturalization process.

Passenger lists are a good source to find your ancestor coming across the big pond. It can take hours upon hours going through many lists to find them. You will need to know about what year they immigrated to make your search easier. Remember when searching through ship lists that your ancestor may have traveled back and forward to their country. Just like today we visit friends and family and so did they.

CHAPTER VI

ALMSHOUSE, ORPHANS, WORKHOUSE & POORHOUSE RECORDS

Workhouses were popular in European countries. Some felt the workhouses were a good place as they had shelter, food and a place to work. People were starving and so they went to the workhouses. The truth of the matter is people were abused and died every day.

Along with men and women there were children also present in the workhouses. They came with their families, they came because they were orphans, they came because they were crippled, and they came and suffered. The workhouse did have schools to educate the children. The girls were used for domestic help and the boys did local work.

The smaller children who were infants to 5 years of age were all placed in one room and never were taken outside to play or to get a bit of fresh air. Many children were subjected to beatings for disobeying or breaking the rules. It is no wonder with the stories coming out of these workhouses the Irish people feared them.

In 1800 many immigrants were poor and when they came to the US they found themselves in city Almshouses.

Almshouse is a place for the homeless. These Almshouses date back to Colonial times. They also included people who were not only poor but were blind, deaf and dumb, mentally retarded, aged, unmarried mothers and unwanted children.

These places offered people food, clothing, and medical care. In return they were subjected to hard labor. They were not nice places to live when there was a lack of funding and many finally closed.

Olivetree.com allows you to search Almshouse, Orphans and Poorhouse records in New York City, NY from 1819-1840.

What you will find in these records is the date of admission, name, age, country of origin, time of arrival; port sailed from, port of arrival, and name of ship. As you can see if you find your ancestor in these records you will learn a lot about where they came from. Sometimes you will also find information about their death or an illness they may have had.

Poor farms were popular in the 1800s. People would live and work on these farms. They were run by the town or the county for the poor. These poorhouses or farms were mainly found in the US but Canada also started using this system.

There are sometimes cemeteries connected to these poorhouses. Later in the 1900s some of these places became homes for the aged.

Almshouses started in Europe developed by churches and date back as far as the 1500s. Another country that had Almshouses was in Norway and they were developed around 1270.

The first Almshouse in the US was in the town of Boston in 1622. William Penn brought the traditional English Almshouse to America. There are many stories of the people being whipped and mistreated. They were sad places but for the poor and disabled it was their only help.

Orphanages were developed in the US in the early 1700s in New Orleans. Children were abandoned by their parents or they lost their parents through death. As immigration increased so did orphan children. Many children lost parents due to accident or illness and because the parents could not afford to raise and feed their children due to bad times. Your ancestor may have become an orphan due to cholera, tuberculosis or influenza that caused the death of one or more parent that developed in their town.

If you are searching for someone in an orphanage it will be a hard task. You will need to learn the history of the orphanages in the area you are researching. You can use paid websites like the one below.

DNA testing is a good way to trace down an orphan in your family.

https://www.olivetreegenealogy.com/orphans/

Many times you are unable to find your ancestor and they could be hiding in a hospital and asylum records. Sadly hospitals only retain their records for a short period of time. Also many times the hospital may have closed depending on how long ago. You can find these records through state and local historical societies.

Genealogy trails is one place you can search for these records.

www.genealogytrials.com

Digital public library of America is another place you can look. Just type in "Hospital Records".

https://dp.la/

CHAPTER VII

CHURCH RECORDS

Many churches keep records on vital statistics like birth, baptismal, marriage, deaths, and burial. You will have to locate the parish/church in the neighborhood where your ancestor lived. Look on birth record, marriage, or burial records and see who the priest or reverend was on the document. Many times in an obituary it will mention the church or clergyman.

Church records can many times give us relationships to family members. You will also need to know the religion of the family. Don't just assume because your family is Catholic now that they always were years back. In some cases families changed their religion for various reasons.

If your family was Baptist, take a look at American Baptist Historical Society. http://baptisthistoryhomepage.com/

The Catholic Church records contain the same records as most other churches but may have better and more extensive records. You will have to contact the diocese for the church if it has closed records. You can sometimes find these records in civil archives, universities or the historical society. Familyseach.org will have many records along with a paid site Ancestry.com. You can contact the parish priest who will sometimes be helpful.

Many people were buried in their parish cemetery so it could be another good source. Many children went to Catholic schools which can add to your research. Your family may have those records that could have additional information for your research. At present all records for the Catholic Church are at the diocesan archives.

Lutheran records can be found at: http://genealoger.com/lutheran/luth_church_records.htm

There you will find churches by state. As for all religious records you can search paid and free websites.

Quaker records for New York and the Pennsylvania area are housed at Swarthmore College in their historical library and Haverford College in Pennsylvania. The Indiana Historical Society also houses these records.

Quaker website https://www.swarthmore.edu/friends-historical-library

Mennonite and Amish offer a great research site online. You can search at: http://mcusa-archives.org/MennObits/index.html Just click on the index pages.

I think the bottom line is no matter what religion your family was always, look at all the churches in the area where your family lived. Many times a couple who married could be from different faiths. The groom could be Protestant while the bride was Catholic. One thing you will not find is records before 1700.

In searching these church records you could get lucky. Sometimes the church kept records of the member who attended previous churches. If that was across the pond you will now have important immigration records

You have to remember county lines changed through the years and though your family may have lived in Spotsylvania County, Virginia in 1721 it became Orange County in 1734.

Probably the best place to search for your ancestor's records would be the family history library in Utah. You can use www.Google.com to find books written about the area where they lived.

Church newsletters are another source in finding additional information. Many times it will tell about the member and what is going on in their lives. It can also tell you when members leave the church and moved to another state or town.

Many times books are written listing marriage and other vital information for certain counties and state. Look on Google books and search to see if there is a book on the town where your folks lived. Also check libraries in those areas as they may have a book mentioning marriage, etc in the town.

 For instance I own two books on marriages for Orange County, Virginia. One is Marriages of Orange County Virginia 1747-1810. The other book is Marriage records of the city of Fredericksburg, and of Orange, Spotsylvania and Stafford counties, Virginia 1722-1850. The later one I purchased from Heritage Book, Inc., which is a great place to find genealogical books.

In early days there may have only been one church in the town so that is where everyone attended no matter what religion they were.

Don't be afraid to contact the church and see if the records exist. Some church records are published in books. There are a lot of records being placed on microfilm and housed at historical societies. Check all libraries and societies your ancestor lived near and see if they have any church records. Some church records are on http://www.newhorizonsgenealogicalservices.com/church-records.htm.

German church records are important in your German research as they provide lineage. Most birth, marriage and death civil records are not available before 1871, so church records are important.

Some church records can date back to the 1400s, though most started around 1550. Catholic churches began keeping records around 1545 and Protestant are before that date.

Marriage records were usually in the bride's church. If a woman was a widow and married again she would use her deceased husband's surname.

Deaths were also recorded and can be found in the Knell book. This book recorded the tolling of the bell, which was the third day after the death.

There are many languages found written in German church records. They are handwritten and sometimes hard to read.

England required all churches to keep records starting in 1538 and in 1754 they started keeping marriages and banns in a printed form.

Looking at other countries like Norwegians parish records didn't start until the mid 1600s. Priests kept records of baptismal, marriages and funerals. Their records are kept at the National Archives Regional Repositories.

French vital records were recorded starting in 1792. Baptismal and burial records were kept by the church in 1539. You will need to know the town your ancestor lived in as there is no index.

Norway has the bygdeboker, village books. They were commissioned by the municipality and were written by the people. These books can hold information about church records, census, and listing farm owners. You can find these at the National Archives.

Spain started recording baptismal in 1497. Belgium National Archives hold records from churches. Brazil civil records started about 1875 and Chile started right after in 1885.

New Zealand records began in 1848 but there is a limit of 100 years for births, stillborns 50 years and marriages 80 years. Deaths had to be 80 years from a person's birth date.

Every church and country had their own set of rules in recording vital records.

CHAPTER VIII

CEMETERY RECORDS

If you are looking for where your ancestor was buried I would first start with Find A Grave. https://www.findagrave.com/

With Find a Grave you can search by entering the name and it will bring up all the people with that name from all over the world. Entering the town or state is also very helpful and any additional information you may have.

Churches are one of the best places to look. In many places around the world you will find cemeteries connected to a church. National cemeteries of Fallen Soldiers are another place to look.

 At cemeteries you can find occupations, members of an organization, children's names, and additional family names. Many people write interesting things on their tombstones that can tell you about the person. Many times lost children you didn't know of will be found buried with a parent.

Let's not forget the memorials around the world that lists names of people who are found in memorials like the Vietnam Wall or Notre Dame de Lorette cemetery in France where 40,000 French soldiers are buried. WWI and WWII memorials hold information about your ancestor if they fought in those wars.

If you don't know where they were buried then you will have to determine where it may be. You can check death certificates that give the cemetery or obits in the newspaper that also may give that information. Military records are another place to find these records. If the cemetery isn't listed in the record then try the undertaker who may be listed on an obituary. Find the phone number and give him a call. Some historical societies may have listings of very early undertakers and who they buried. You can also check the census records you last saw them in before they dropped off the census and put that location in your search on Find a Grave with the town and state last listed.

Once you locate the cemetery there is a lot of information available on these records. Don't be afraid to call the cemetery to see if they have any additional information on your ancestor. They will sometimes have plot information with other relative's burial locations. People many times would buy multiple plots for family members. Families would tend to use the same funeral home and cemetery. In my case my ancestor's tombstone displayed a military emblem for the GAR which led me to additional information about him. Many times tombstones will connect you with other family members mentioned on their stone. The Gar is the Grand Army of the Republic and was a fraternal order which was veterans from the Union Army, US Navy, Marines and the US Revenue Cutter Service who served during the Civil War.

Funeral home records have a lot of information that is missed in searches. You will find a person's name, relatives' names, date of birth and death, occupation and military service. Sometimes funeral homes go out of business and you can find records at libraries and societies.

If you can locate someone at the cemetery make sure you walk around and keep your eyes open as there could be an ancestor buried close by.

The mid 1800s many times funeral homes were not used and they used their homes and were buried quickly. You may even find information in probate records as the funeral was paid for through the will.

The real stumbling block is when the cemetery has been moved. You will have to find out where it was relocated.

Here is a website for Pennsylvania cemeteries-
http://www.daddezio.com/cemetery/junction/CJ-PA-001.html

The Catholic Cemetery Association

http://www.ccapgh.org/cemeteries.asp

This website will give you cemeteries around the world with lists of persons buried in the cemetery. This is a wonderful source.

http://www.interment.net/cemetery.htm

Here is a list of Americans who died and are buried in Cemeteries and Memorials throughout the world.

Ardennes American Cemetery and Memorial- Belgium

St. James American Cemetery- France- Normandy Invasion

Brookwood American Cemetery and Memorial- British Isles- WWI

Cambridge American Cemetery- England

Epinal American Cemetery and Memorial- France- WWII

Flanders Field American Cemetery and Memorial- Belgium- WWI

Florence American Cemetery and Memorial- Florence, Italy- the fifth Army

Hendri- Chapelle American Cemetery and Memorial- Belgium- WWII

Lorraine American Cemetery and Memorial- France WWII

Luxenbourgh American Cemetery and Memorial-Luxenbourgh- Battle of the Bulge

Manilla American Cemetery and Memorial- Phillippines-WWII

Muse-Argonne American Cemetery and Memorial- France- WWI

CHAPTER IX

HISTORICAL SOCIETIES AND LIBRARIES

Historical Societies and Libraries are a wonderful resource for records. Start first with their card catalog. Some are actual card files you look in and are arranged alphabetically. Many libraries have them on a computer database for easy look-up.

You can find very old documents. Some historical libraries will contain books written on certain surnames and will include all generations.

In looking at very old documents an archivists will bring the document to you and after putting on gloves you can look at the document. At that time you will be given instructions on how to handle the document.

Historical Societies and libraries also have microfilm and microfiche that you can search through for specific sources such as newspaper articles, etc.

Very early birth, death and marriage records are housed at the historical society for the area they are in, also land records and information about neighborhoods and maps.

Many times libraries offer classes on genealogy and you can learn what is available. You can find state censuses at most libraries but they will probably be on microfilm. You can even find biographies or memoirs. Old newspapers are a wealth of information that may be on microfilm.

Maps can be an important research tool that will show you where buildings are located. They also may have books written about the history of the town or an event that happened there where your ancestor was mentioned. These all may seem like little bits of research but when you hit that brick wall they can be invaluable. Many times county lines changed over the years and you can look at county maps to see where those lines changed.

Don't forget colleges and university libraries. Swarthmore college library is one of the best places to look for an ancestor who was a Quaker. Not to mention Virginia library, this is very important to folks looking for their Virginia ancestors.

Some of the things found in libraries are newspaper articles, maps, magazines, books on the local area. One of the best kept secrets is you can access paid genealogy databases for free. Many like Ancestry, Fold3 and My Heritage are accessible through libraries. Also eBooks are available through your libraries. Unfortunately not all libraries offer this opportunity but make sure you check to see if your library has this great offer.

If you can travel or live near these genealogy libraries you should try to visit as they have a wealth of information. Here is a list below.

Make sure when you go bring your information with you either in folders or on your computer. Many libraries allow you to plug in while doing your research.

Also found in libraries are biographies, memoirs and old newspapers.

Family History Library, Salt Lake City, Utah

Allen County Public Library, Indiana

The Daughters of the American Revolution, Washington, DC

Midwest Genealogy Center, Missouri

Clayton Library Center, Houston, Texas

New England Historic Genealogical Society's Library, Boston, Massachusetts

Also don't forget your local libraries as they are a good starting point.

Many counties have transferred older records to libraries, historical societies and archives.

Allen County Public Library

http://www.acpl.lib.in.us/home/research

Follow the page to research and then page down to genealogy. There you can place in the search space a name or topic.

Join an ethnic genealogical Society

Subscribe to Family Tree Magazine.

Worldcat- It is the world's largest card catalog which lists libraries around the world. You can search through their collections of books many who may have your family.

www.worldcat.org/

Smithsonian libraries- you can search by author or subject. Some books can be read online or downloaded.

https://library.si.edu/

Google books-I can't tell you how many ancestors I have found through this site in books. Make sure you do advanced search

www.book.google.com

CHAPTER X

INTERNATIONAL RECORDS

Have you tried WIKI at familysearch.com? It has a great search engine which you can search by place or topic. There you enter what you're looking for and it brings up amazing information. In my case I put in Ireland resources. What I got was all kinds of records for Ireland. This is what I found. Irish schools, Ireland Civil Registrations, maps, church records, taxation, a list of county information, and Irish census. There were over 500 listings just for Ireland.

All paid websites are very helpful in searching for international records. Of course you can travel the country your ancestor is from but you better have a lot of information before you get there. Newspapers will post arrivals and is a good source for immigration records.

One problem people have in getting birth records from another country is the names may not be written in English. Some are written in Latin. Here is a website that shows Latin names with the English counterpart.

https://en.wiktionary.org/wiki/Appendix:Latin_forms_of_English_given_names

Searching WIKI can be very helpful. Place a nationality or country in the search record for instance place Hispanic or English in doing your search. There are National Archives in other countries. Search them out. One problem could be that they are not written in English.

Find my Past is another paid site that is useful in looking for international records. https://www.findmypast.com/

WorldGenWeb Project is another website to look at. http://worldgenweb.org/. You can search all over the world.

 Make sure you learn about the habits of the people and history of the country. In this case look at the famine records and different wars during the time your ancestor lived there if your ancestors are from Ireland.

If you are looking for tax records in other countries you can find some at Familysearch.com. You must search under collections and then tax. Land records are also available there.

Here are some places to look for records.

England, Scotland, Wales and Ireland

I will try and represent as many countries as I possibly can to give you insight in searching for your ancestors abroad. I did not include websites where the language isn't in English.

One thing you may want to keep in mind is naming pattern. Scotland and Ireland both have them and though they don't always apply it sometimes does and helps in finding your ancestor. Not all families followed this tradition, though.

Scotland naming patterns

First son- paternal grandfather

Second son- maternal grandfather

Third son- father

Fourth and all children after- father or mother's brother

First daughter- maternal grandmother

Second daughter- paternal grandmother

Third Daughter-mother

Daughters were generally named after mother's and father's sisters

Irish naming patterns

First son- paternal grandfather

Second son- maternal grandfather

Third son- father

Fourth son- father's eldest brother

First Daughter- maternal grandmother

Second Daughter-father's mother

Third Daughter- mother

Fourth Daughter- mother's eldest sister

All England census records are from 1841 to 1911. All censuses that were taken after 1911 are closed for 100 years. You can view these census records online at the National Archives.

http://www.nationalarchives.gov.uk/ and through paid site Findmypast.co.uk (1901-1911) and Ancestry.co.uk (1841, 1851, 1861, 1871, 1881, and 1891)

Free BMD- Civil Registration Index- it will give you marriages and deaths for England & Wales-www.familydaily.com

Free UK Census- www.ukcensusonline.com/ includes census from 1841, 1851, 1861, 1871, 1881, 1891, 1901, 1911 and 1921

Another source for records is:

shttps://www.ukbmd.org.uk/county/yorkshire/parish_records/
This will give a source for birth, marriage and death records for Yorkshire Parish, England.

GENUKI is a library of genealogical information

GENUKI Ireland, GENUKI England, and GENUKI Scotland are free index searches. You will find birth, death, marriage, and census. You must first login or register.

GENUKI England and Wales you can search all records plus counties.

Ireland

In Ireland the most complete census is 1901 & 1911 but there are partial census from 1821-1851. What you will find in these is name, head of household, county, district, electoral division, townland, and street. Searching any ancestor in another country can be difficult. Here are some places you can search to help in your research. Most times your ancestor will be listed in the census as farmer or laborer which is the same occupation. They usually were tenant farmers and didn't own the land but rented from a landlord. Griffith's Valuation is a good place to start. When a person was omitted from it they have usually died. You can find additional information at the National Library of Ireland.

The Tithe Applotment books give good information of the poor in Ireland. It gives the tax each occupier had to pay. Clergy did not have to pay this tax. What you will find in the records is the name of occupier, townland, amount of acreage, and amount to pay. Here is the link to search the Tithe Appotment. http://titheapplotmentbooks.nationalarchives.ie/search/tab/home.jsp

www.proni.com - Public Record Office of Northern Ireland.

Here you will find church records, valuation books & maps, Tithe Allotment books, estate records, school records, Will records, guardian records and hospital records.

Donegal Genealogy Resources- www.donegalgenealogy.com

Catholic Parish Registers at NLI - https://registers.nli.ie/

Donegal County Council

http://www.donegalcoco.ie/culture/archives/digitisedarchives/

Here you can search by entering the parish your ancestor was from and you will find baptismal and marriages.

National Archive -http://discovery.nationalarchives.gov.uk/

http://www.rootsireland.ie/ - This is a paid site

Irish Immigration database

http://www.dippam.ac.uk/

Learn about the famine at Doagh Famine Village

http://www.doaghfaminevillage.com/attractions/

If you want to write for birth, marriage and death records for Ireland you can do so at the address below.

North Western Health Board
Superintendant Registrar of birth, death and marriage
Tirconnail, Letterkenny, Ireland

Irish birth, marriage and death records start in 1864 for Catholic records, and 1845 for non Catholic.

Scotland

The National records of Scotland

https://www.nrscotland.gov.uk/

They have 100 year privacy for their census. Census records are from 1841 forward every ten years. There is no census for the years 1941 and 1966. The 1921 census will be released in 2021.

National Records of Scotland- www.nrscotland.gov.uk/

One of the best kept secrets for Scottish records is the tax records which are also known as the Clock and Watch tax rolls of 1797 to 1798. www.bespokegenealogy.com/

If you are looking for newspaper records go to The Glasgow Herald. Do a Google search and you will find a newspaper section from 1806-1990.

Census records for Scotland

https://www.nrscotland.gov.uk/research/guides/census-records#open census records

1841 Census you will find name and occupation, age is rounded off to nearest five for anyone over 15 years old, yes or no if the person was born in Scotland

1851 Census you will find the Street they lived on, name of person at that address, relationship to head of household, age, occupation, where they were born.

1861 Census they added the number of children over the ages 5 to 15 attending school and number of rooms with one or more windows.

1871 Census not any new additions except if the person was deaf, blind, dumb, idiotic or lunatic.

1881 Census they added status of marriage, and were you a Gaelic speaking person

1891 Census no real changes

1901 Census if you were born in a foreign country

1911 Census the question on disability was changed, occupation was extended, and place of birth was extended.

A great place for Scottish ancestors

https://www.scotlandspeople.gov.uk/

Germany

You first have to establish when your ancestor was born in Germany. Just like all people searching their foreign ancestors it is best to look at immigration records as we discussed in chapter 5. Another means is ships lists, court records, church records and cemetery records in the US. Just as you were to search for a job you begin networking with other people this method works the same way. Get your ancestor out there and put them on every message board and social media board. On paid sites they usually have a network system to talk to other people, too.

A great place to search your German ancestry is familysearch.org as it is free. After entering the site look at the top of the page for search, if you click on it you will be given a pull down menu. Click on search WIKI. It will then give you a search box that you can enter place or topic. Enter Germany or any other country you are searching. There you will find all the tools you need to search for you ancestor in Germany and any other country. What I found was German research tools, records, history of the country, maps and German jurisdictions in English and German.

AFRICA

Search out Africa Gen Web Project at www.africagenweb.com/

AUSTRALIA

National Archives of Australia can be found at:

http://www.aa.gov.au/. Here you will find all the information you need to obtain records and do your research in Australia.

Queenstown National Archives can be found at:

https://www.qld.gov.au/dsiti/qsa

BELGIUM/NETHERLANDS

http://www.arch.be/index.php?l=en&m=genealogist

http://www.french-genealogy.typepad.com/genealogie/2013/03/finding-your-anco-belgfrian-ancestors-just-got-easier.html

CANADA

http://www.bac-lac.gc.ca/eng/discover/genealogy/Pages/introduction.aspx

http://www.genealogysearch.org/canada/

CHINA

Chinese genealogy- http://www.legacy1.net/

CUBA

The Cuban genealogy Club of Miami- https://cubangenclub.org/

CZECH REPUBLIC

Czech Genealogy and Heraldry Society in Prague

http://www.genealogie.cz/en/

DENMARK

Dansk Demografisk Database

http://www.ddd.dda.dk/ddd_en.htm

FINLAND

The History of Finland- https://histdoc.net/history/history.html

FRANCE

American-French Genealogical Society- http://afgs.org/site/

GREECE

Greek Genealogy- http://www.daddezio.com/grekgen.html

HUNGARY

Hungarian and Slovak Genealogy

http://www.dholmes.com/hafs.html

Hungarian Jewish Genealogy-
https://www.jewishgen.org/Hungary/

ITALY

Italian Genealogy- https://www.italiangenealogy.com/

Sicily genealogy- http://www.angelfire.com/mt/sicily1/

INDIA

http://forebears.io/india

NEW ZEALAND

New Zealand Genealogy-
http://www.genealogylinks.net/newzealand/

NORWAY

Norwegian Historical Data Center-
http://www.rhd.uit.no/indexeng.html

POLAND

Polish Genealogical Society of America- https://pgsa.org/

Polish Genealogical Society of Michigan- https://pgsm.org/

Online Records for Poland-
http://www.lostshoebox.com/poland/online-records/

SWEDEN

https://www.arkivdigital.net/swedish-genealogy

http://swedishgenealogyguide.com/archives/tag/swedish-birth-record

RUSSIA

https://www.familysearch.org/wiki/en/Russia_Online_Genealogy_Records

So you found a document from another country and it is written in their language so what do you do? Go to this website and type in the language you need and it will translate for you.

https://translate.google.com

CHAPTER XI

TAX AND LAND RECORDS

Several things that you will find in land records is your ancestor, their location and timeline. It will also give you neighbors who may be related. Tax records are a valuable source and are very accurate. In colonial times there were tax collectors. You can learn about real estate, personal property, occupation and businesses through tax records. There are many tax records you can look at. Poll, real estate, property, federal, inheritance, and school tax all places to look for tax records. You can find ages, residence and relationships through tax records.

Don't forget to look for these records in grantee and grantor indexes, homestead applications and water rights. Keep in mind the county lines changed over time. Many merged with other counties. Make yourself a map and show where the county lines changed over time. If you don't pay attention to this you may miss a record because it is in another county.

All the states have an officer that handles assessment of properties. You may find them under assessor, auditor, county clerk, treasurer or real property taxation. You can find these records online by state.

Some taxes in Colonial times were called quit rent, tithables, and poll or head tax. Persons were taxed from age 16 to 60 years old. Veterans and ministers were not taxed. The government started taxing in 1798 and these records can be found at State historical societies. County clerks hold local tax records.

My ancestor was on a 1704 Quit Rent Roll for King and Queen County, Va. He owned 150 acres. The Basic English land laws under which American colonists gained title to their land required owners to pay the Crown or proprietor a Quit Rent based on the number of acres of land owned.

You can find land tax records on a paid site like Ancestry.com. There you will find databases like land tax records from 1692-1932. What you would find in these records is property owners and tenants, county and parish, and year.

The names listed as witnesses in deeds and legal documents were close friends or family members. They can even be brother-in-laws and sister-in-laws.

In the State of Virginia the colonists didn't have enough laborers to work on their farms. The Virginia Company of London offered investors shares in their company and in return they received land.

In 1618 the headright system was developed and each planter was awarded 100 acres of land who had lived in the colony since 1616. It also gave 50 acres to each person who paid the cost of transporting a person to America. This system in time became corrupt.

Apprentice records are able to be found due to the Stamp Act of 1709 when there was a tax on the indenture. Apprenticeship started as far back as the 1100s. In the 1700s this was a popular way for folks to have their passage paid. It stills goes on today but in a different way.

They learn their trade and received food and shelter. Before they left their mother country they signed a contract for 7 years which bound them to a tradesman. This wasn't just for the poor. Many young folks learned their trade in this manner. Parents would send their children to another family/tradesman to learn their skill. Many times it was just so they would learn how to run a farm.

Sometimes these apprenticeships weren't all they were cracked up to be and became hard to endure so they fled. You can sometimes find newspaper ads in an older paper advertising a runaway. They had made an investment in this person and want to get their return.

 What you will find in these apprentice records are name, address and parents names. In some cases each apprentice received $50 upon arrival. The best place to find these records is at a paid website FindMyPast.com.

The indentured servants unlike the apprentices didn't learn a trade but they were transported by a person and were in their service for 4-7 years.

HERE IS AN ENTRY IN THE CAVALIER AND PIONEER PATENT BOOK. AS YOU CAN SEE ROBERT CLERKE RECEIVED 50 ACRES FOR EACH PERSON HE TRANSPORTED FOR A TOTAL OF 2000 ACRES . This was a very profitable business.

"CAVALIERS AND PIONEERS PATENT BOOK No. 4; Pg 366
ROBERT CLERKE, 2000 acs. upon a creek issuing out of Petomeck freshes above the narrowes at Puscatoway which divides this from a tract aperteining to John Wood, Rob. Smith & John Ayres. 15 July 1657, p. 173, (259). Trans. of 40 pers.• "

Business merchants would collect these headright certificates and sell them. These records are found in Cavaliers and Pioneers, Abstracts of Virginia Land Patents and Grants, 1623-1666, Virginia Gleaning in England, Quit Rents of Virginia, Library of Virginia Land Office Grants and Virginia Northern Neck Land Grants.

During the 1800s Australia offered settlers limited squatter land leases for 14 years. They would even pay for their fares so they would set up farms.

Newspapers are a good source for these records. A tax list was placed in the newspaper yearly in some locations. When checking tax records in a county it can also tell you when your ancestor arrived from another country or if they moved. When your ancestor is absent from the tax record there is a good chance he is deceased. Keep looking in county courthouses, historical societies, state and national archives for these records and you may find your elusive ancestor.

Deeds date back to the Revolutionary War. You will have to look for a deed in the state where it was filed. Each state is different in where deeds are found. Some can be found in courthouses and others in state archives.

The legal age for someone to own land was 21 years old so if you find your ancestor owning land you will know he was 21 years or older. You can look for tax records in county courthouses, county historical societies, state archives. You can find Virginia tax records at:

http://www.binnsgenealogy.com/

Familysearch.com has United States Internal Revenue Assessment Lists from 1862-1874 when you go to "Search" and then "Records" on their site. You can also find these records on paid websites like Ancestry.com.

Many times parents transferred land to their children. General Land Office Records from the Bureau of Land Management is a great source to start. You can search at the website https://glorecords.blm.gov/default.aspx.

If your ancestors were living in the eastern states use the Bureau of Land Management and the National Archives for the eastern states.

Eastern State Office, Bureau of Land Management
Dept. of Interior
20 M Street, Suite 950 Washington, DC 20003

Another type of land record is land patents. They are a legal document which transfers land from the US government to individuals. What you will find in these records is age, place of birth, citizenship and military service.

These records can give additional information on your ancestor like age, place of birth and military service. You can order land entry records with form NATF 84 and can be ordered online at National Archives. You can search these records at the Bureau of Land Management.

www.glorecords.blm.gov

The Military Bounty Land Warrants were before 1908 and allowed veterans who serviced in the Military to claim land in the northwest and western territories. He had to apply for the warrant and then was given a land patent which allowed him ownership of that property. Deeds are one way to find a spouse as they are usually listed. You can find deed books in county clerks offices. This is a great way to trace the land your ancestors owned and track where they may have gone.

Land records in some states are in the State Archives, which are land entry case files. Tract books which are land entry case files for Eastern states. They are available at the National Archives for Eastern tract books you can write to:

Eastern State Office, Bureau of Land Management
Dept of Interior
20 M Street, Suite 950
Washington, DC 20003

City Directories are one of the places you can find your ancestor if he/she didn't own property. If you are looking in another country for tax records or land records some are available on familysearch.com and Ancestry.com and other paid sites.

On familysearch.com if you get on WIKI you can enter "land records" in search. This will bring up land records all over the world. You can search by state, also.

Virginia land patents started in 1606 when the Virginia Company of London granted settlers land patents until 1623. From 1618-1732 headrights were grants given 50 acres of land per person which could be himself, wife, servant, slave or passenger. You can find these grants in a book Cavaliers & Pioneers: Abstracts of Virginia patents and land grants by Nell Marion Nugent.

In New York you will find land papers from 1643-1676 Colonial Patents and Land Grants at the National Archive which are searchable there. Pennsylvania records can be found also at the

State Archives and Pennsylvania Historical and Museum Commission website. The State Archive also has images of Warrant Registers from 1733-1957 that includes every county in Pennsylvania.

You can find each state's land records through WIKI at familysearch.com.

Did you ever wonder what your grandparent's house looked like in its day? Google Earth has a feature that allows you to go back as far as 1950. You may only be able to find these homes in well populated areas, though. Depending on the area and home you can even go back to the 1800s.

If you would like to try this out go to: https://www.historicaerials.com/

There is a fee.

CHAPTER XII

PROBATE RECORDS

Wills can be chock full of information about our ancestors. If you can't find other vital information in a will you could hit the jackpot. With a will your ancestor is explaining who and what he wants to do with his estate. It is filed in the courthouse in the state in which he lived. It will give you the property and land including his heirs and guardians. It can also show a list of creditors and debt.

In inventory you will find all items owned by that individual and give you a picture of how he lived. It will be a list of every item and the value of each.

If children are involved a guardianship will be made. This sets up someone such as a friend or family member to care for the minor children. It will name each child and this is a record that can be very helpful in finding children.

You will need to know the state and county where your ancestor lived in looking for their will. Men and women made wills in colonial times and to this day. When I was looking for my many great grandfathers wills I came across a will for one of his children's husbands. In his will he named his wife Mary and the land that was left to her from her father Roger. Right there it gave me Mary's maiden name and who her father was. This was valuable information as this will was from the 1700s and vital information was scarce.

Sometimes it is difficult to understand written wills so here are some items you will see in wills.

PRIMOGENITURE- the oldest son inherits the entire estate. If there were no sons then the daughters would share equally.

DOWER- Is for the widow to care for herself and their children. The widow also receives 1/3 of all the land her husband owned.

INTERSTATE- Indicates someone who dies without a will. The courts will distribute the person's assets.

TESTATE- left a will.

EXECUTOR- someone who may have to post bond to make sure they fulfill their duties.

What you will find in a will is name, death date, residence, administrator of will, marital status, spouse, children who are usually named in birth order, spouses of daughters, grandchildren, witnesses, a " X" mark if he/she couldn't write, where they owned land and possibly their occupation, and date filed. Not all wills give you all the information you are looking for but are still a good source.

Fathers usually left the family farm to the eldest son so he may not be mentioned in the will. Sons are named first in the will and by birth status. Daughters are named second. If a daughter is married she will be named as my daughter Mary Bell, wife of Edward Smith. This is now our record that Mary Bell was married to Edward Smith on the date of the will.

If there was some friction between a parent and child they may only leave them a very small amount of money which could be less than a dollar. If a child has died than the parent may leave their inheritance to the grandchildren. Always check Aunts and Uncles wills as they could lead to additional records of the family.

If you are looking for a copy of your family member's will all probate records are public. You will need to go to the circuit court, surrogate court or orphan court. In my case I lived in the county of my ancestor and I made a phone call to the appropriate court and told them who I was looking for. They in turn looked up to see if there was in fact a will for my ancestor. There was and so they quoted me the cost to receive the will and the date I could pick it up. It was a very simple process.

Wills are a great place for African Americans to find their family. In colonial times when a will was made the people named in the will were important in their lives and property they owned. Slaves were one of those important people. The person is usually listed by their first name but if you add the surname of the person who wrote the will then you just may have the full name of your ancestor. Keep in mind that all slaves weren't freed until December 1865 after the Civil War. Pair this up with the slave schedule censuses from 1850 and 1860 which listed enslaved people by gender, age and race can add to your success.

Check census records after 1865 and you may find your ancestor living free with their other family members that were once slaves in the household of the plantation owner. Also keep in mind their ages as you look through the two records though there could be a slight difference.

Remember there weren't only colored slaves there were white slaves also Irish white slaves were brought over for many reasons. There were also indentured slaves. People could not afford to pay for their passage so they became indentured servants. An indentured servant is when a person pays for your passage to come to America. They are given a specific number of years, usually 4 to 7 years, to work for that person. Once your time is completed you are freed. Irish slavery began in the mid 1600s. They were men, women and children shipped from Britain to America. All of these activities were eventually abolished.

There are several places you can search for your ancestor's will. Paid sites are very good and free sites can also be utilized like familysearch.org. You can search by name but it may be easier to search first by CATALOG then SUBJECT and finally by COUNTRY. Make sure you type in the word PROBATE in SUBJECT. If you are only searching within the US at familysearch.org website then just click SEARCH and go to the far right you will see a map of the world. Below that you will see FIND A COLLECTION. Type in the word PROBATE and then it will bring up the states in alphabetical order. Let's say we go to Pennsylvania which shows us that the records for wills are from 1683-1994. You will have to browse through 3,200,560 images. They are listed by county in the state. For example, I clicked on Chester County and they were listed by will date and estate date. You will then have to work through the original images for you ancestor.

PRONI is a website where you can find Wills for Northern Ireland. Once you are on the website you will see WILL CALENDARS after you click on that it will bring you to SEARCH WILL CALENDARS to the right page down to the green box that says WILL CALENDAR. You will then be asked to enter the name of the person and additional information if you have it.

English wills are found at Somerset House in London and before 1858 you will find them in Ecclesiastical courts by county. Prerogative Court of Canterbury had a jurisdiction over England and Wales. People in the northern counties used the Prerogative Court of York.

French wills are found at the notaries. Wills that are over 125 years old are found at the Regional Archives or Nation Archives.

Canadian wills are found in a probate court

Italian wills are found at the notaries and are found at the State Archives, local courts, National Archives or the town Registry Office.

German wills are found at District Court Houses or State Archives.

All countries have wills and are sometimes difficult to find. Paid websites are sometimes the best place to search. Not all wills are filed as soon as the person dies so keep an open mind and look for years passed the death date.

This is a website you can search for items listed below and obtain copies of those records. Here is the website.
http://www.sampubco.com

Wills and Heirs

Surrogate's Records/Probate/Estate Files

Guardianship

Naturalization

Misc. Orders and Decrees

Letters of Administration

Letters of Testamentary

Petitions of Administration

Proof of Will

Cemetery Burials

Renunciations

Biographies

CHAPTER XIII

MESSAGE BOARDS AND SOCIAL MEDIA

Message boards are a great place to talk to people looking for the same information. There you can research questions that other people have already posted and you can search a certain topic or surname you are looking for. You may find information you were looking for, but you have to keep in mind that unless it is a document they are posting or where you can find the document then you will need to do your own verification.

Ancestry.com message boards you can search for context within the message board which includes surnames and specific topics under surnames. You have the ability to search countries or other categories like cemeteries or tombstones. It will all contain messages about a specific subject. When searching surnames you can enter " S" surname that way if there is a difference or alternate spelling of the name search the site and you can find it. If you search only your surname then you will find every message written about that surname and the person who wrote the message. This gives you the advantage to make contact with other people searching for the same surname.

You can also place your own message on these boards.

GenForum message board here again you type in the surname and receive all messages with that surname. After you read the messages and you feel there is a connection you can then reply.

When replying to any message you should make sure you give as much information about your ancestor as you can. Too many times while trying to help someone I have come across people who only gave limited information. After I had spent an hour trying to help, the information I found was already in the hands of the person asking for the help. Also people will pass by your message if they don't see enough information. If you just don't have any more information just say so.

Rootsweb message board is another place you can be searching. Works like the rest of the message boards. You can search by name or location.

Facebook can be a resource for finding family. You can join group boards. If you are looking for your Irish roots then you could join YGBW-Genealogy 101. Here you can find marriage records or money saving genealogy sites.

Facebook- Here is a great source for groups you can join

New England Genealogy

Your Genealogy Brick Wall

Midwest Genealogy

Scandinavian Genealogical Research-Center Profession Research

Centre County PA Genealogy

Swiss/Schweiz Genealogy

Sicilian Genealogy, History and Traditions

Ohio Genealogy and History Group

Southwest Oklahoma Genealogy and History Group

Sicilia and Aeolian Island Genealogy

If you have a Facebook page search around and see if you can find one that suits your research.

Newsletters are another great source.

Olivetree.com newsletter- you have to subscribe to the list

Rootsweb.com- has been closed for quite some time and they had a virus. It is not open completely but you can now sign up for the mailing list. Hoping by the time this book is published it will be open and complete as it is a wonderful search engine for records around the world.

Cyndislist.com

Genealogy.com

Eastman's Genealogy newsletter- blog.eogn.com- military genealogy

www.genealogynewsletter.com

www.americanancestors.org- **a weekly e-newsletter**

The New York Genealogical & Biographical Society- FACEBOOK

CHAPTER XIV

FAMILY & RESEARCH CHARTS

Research Checklist

MID-CONTINENT PUBLIC LIBRARY | MIDWEST GENEALOGY CENTER

Name:________________________

Vitals:
Birth:________________ Location:________________
Marriage:________________ Location:________________
Death:________________ Location:________________

US Census Records:
1790:________________ 1870:________________
1800:________________ 1880:________________
1810:________________ 1890:________________
1820:________________ 1900:________________
1830:________________ 1910:________________
1840:________________ 1920:________________
1850:________________ 1930:________________
1860:________________ 1940:________________

State/County Census; Agriculture, Mortality, & Slave Schedules:
____
____
____

Birth Records:
Birth Certificate:________________
Delayed Birth Certificate:________________
Baptism/Christened:________________
Adoption:________________

Death Records:
Death Certificate:________________
Funeral Home:________________
Obituary:________________
Cemetery:________________
Gravestone:________________

Marriage Records:
Marriage Certificate:________________
License:________________
Newspaper:________________
Divorce Decree:________________
Divorce Petition:________________

Military Records:
Branch of Service:________________
Enlistment Card:________________
Wars Fought:________________
Pension Applicaton:________________
Widow's Pension:________________

Probate Records:
Will/Administration:________________
Property Inventory:________________
Guardianship:________________
Estate Sales:________________

Land Records:
Deeds:________________
Abstracts:________________
Plat Map/County Map:________________
Land Patents/Grants:________________

Other Records:
Social Security No.:________________
Church Membership:________________
Family Bible Record:________________
Passenger List:________________
Immigration:________________
Naturalization:________________

City Directories:________________
Voting Records:________________
Tax Lists:________________
Court Records:________________
Children's Vital Records:________________

2

Research Checklist

INDIVIDUAL WORK SHEET

NAME IN FULL: _______________________________   Nickname (AKA): _______________________

BIRTH: Date: _________________________   Christening Date: _______________________
City, County, State: _____________________   City, County, State: ____________________

PARENTS: Father: _________________________   Mother: _________________________________

DEATH: Date: _________________________   Probate: ________________________________
City, County, State: _____________________   Obituary: _______________________________

BURIAL: Date: _________________________   Funeral Home: ___________________________
City, County, State: _____________________   Cemetery: _______________________________

1st MARRIAGE: Date: ______________________   Announcement: ___________________________
City, County, State: _____________________   Place: __________________________________

Spouse: __________________________________   Nickname(AKA): __________________________
Father: __________________________________   Mother: _________________________________

2nd MARRIAGE: Date: ______________________   Announcement: ___________________________
City, County, State: _____________________   Place: __________________________________

Spouse ___________________________________   Nickname (AKA): _________________________
Father: __________________________________   Mother: _________________________________

Immigration/Naturalization: ____
____

Schooling: ____

Religion: ____

Occupations: ____

Military Service: ____

Census Records:
Year   State   County   City   Street
____
____
____
____
____
____
____

Individual Worksheet

Child's Name
Date of Birth
Place of Birth
Mother
Father
Mother's Date & Place of Birth
Father's Date & Place of Birth
Grandmother
Grandmother
Grandfather
Grandfather
My Family History
Sisters' Names
Brothers' Names
MIDWEST GENEALOGY CENTER
06-0027

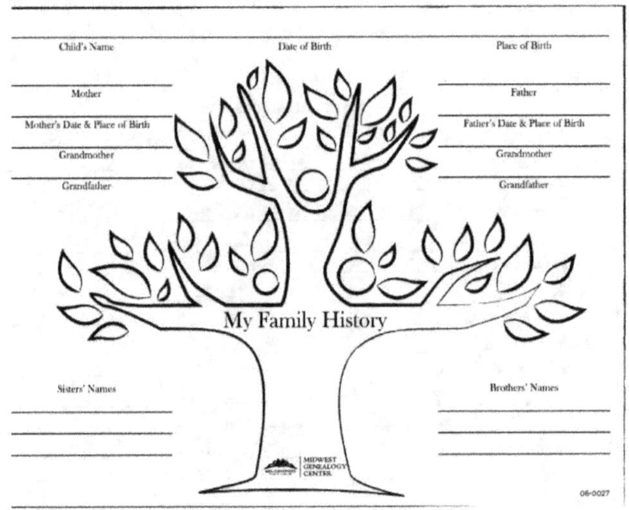

Family Tree

CHAPTER XV

NEWSPAPERS

Searching newspapers can be a wealth of information. Newspapers give you what is going on in the community and the world. They give you a better idea of what was going on during their times and what kind of life they lead. This gives life to your ancestors and allows you to understand their way of living. You must remember just like newspapers today you can find errors in spelling and it just could be your ancestor's name.

I found a newspaper article about my many great grandfathers in Virginia in the 1700s. In it he described a slave who had run away and he had posted a reward for his capture. This newspaper put him at a time and place for me. It also named the slave that could be of help for someone looking for their relative who was a slave in Virginia. Though I'm not proud that my ancestors were slave owners it does help my research on two levels.

In one newspaper I found that the company my great grandfather had worked for honored him and his wife by paying for all his funeral expenses. The article went on to explain where the company was located and what they made along with some wonderful pictures of his place of work. I would have never known any of this if I had not searched for him in the newspapers.

Newspapers also recorded births, marriages and deaths. You can learn about a disaster that may have happened in the town where they lived or an ad for our great grandfather's business. Many times divorces are also entered in newspapers and don't forget the scandals and murders that may have happened. Estate probates are all there in the newspaper. Another thing people miss is school honor rolls which are many times published in newspapers.

Many local libraries will have newspapers you can search on microfilm and historical societies are a good source. Of course you have your paid websites and familysearch.com for free. Here are some of the free sites to access newspapers.

Google News Archives

https://news.google.com/newspapers?hl=en

Chronicling America

https://chroniclingamerica.loc.gov/

Illinois Digital Newspapers Collection

https://digital.library.illinois.edu/collections

Fulton History Old New York Historical Newspaper

https://www.nypl.org/collections/articles-databases/fulton-history-old-new-york-state-historical-newspapers

Historical Newspaper Archives

www.newspapers.com/papers/

Here are some great research sites for Newspapers

Elphind

https://www.veridiansoftware.com/elephind-com/

 Newspapers in many countries

Trove

 https://trove.nla.gov.au/newspaper/?q- Library of Australia

Penn Libraries

 http://viewshare.org/views/refhelp/historical-newspapers-online-usa-2/

ICON International Coalition on Newspapers- Newspaper Digitization Project – list by country
http://icon.crl.edu/digitization.php

Wikipedia List online Newspapers
https://en.wikipedia.org/wiki/Wikipedia:List_of_online_newspaper_archives

Genealogy Bank

www.genealogybank.com

www.newspapers.com

Worldwide Newspaper Collection

www.news.google.com

www.news.google.com/newspapers

CHAPTER XVI

DNA

DNA is the new science in finding your ancestry. Through a bit of salvia you will find out what part of this world you came from and connect with family members. DNA is not enabling you to stop searching for your ancestors. It's a great tool to use with your regular family research. The DAR (Daughters of the American Revolution) has now accepted DNA as evidence of your lineage. I am not an expert on the subject but I will try and give you an overview of what it is and what you will find.

DNA is random and the only people that would have identical DNA would be identical twins. Over two million people have taken the test with Ancestry alone. What they do is they take the DNA from you and match it up with other people who have also taken the test. As you can see the more people who take the test the more results will be available. The accuracy is 98% with any genealogical testing.

Once you receive your raw data from the company you have chosen you can download it to other companies to get better results. It is wise to attach your DNA to your family tree online and if you have not set up a family tree it would be wise to do so. There is a letter at the beginning of your number. This letter is where you had your testing done. (A=Ancestry).

Once your results are in, which takes about 6 to 8 weeks, you will feel lost. You could also find things out that are upsetting like an adoption. Just take it one step at a time and work through it. The ethnicity reports is how they interpreted the results. It is done by computer which compares your information with other population groups.

So which DNA testing company is the best? My Heritage has no privacy concerns while Family Tree DNA is the longest running. You should read about each company and decide which one will give you the results you are looking for in DNA.

Whatever company you choose to use you will have to subscribe to their website to get full results. There are several companies that can test your DNA. Here are the most popular companies: Ancestry DNA, GedMatch DNA, MyHeritage DNA, FamilyTree DNA, and 23 and Me. Here is what you will find in each testing company.

FAMILYTREE DNA

Ancestral report, Cousin matching, 550,00 database, Gedcom upload, Allows Raw DNA download, No privacy concerns, YDNA & MT DNA testing, and Chromosome browsers

MY HERITAGE DNA

Ancestral report, cousin matching, 1 million database, Gedcom upload, Chromosome browser, Allows raw DNA download

Health results and no privacy concerns

ANCESTRY DNA

Ancestral makeup, cousin matching, 6 million database, Gedcom upload, Raw DNA download, Health results, and Privacy concerns Yes

23 AND ME

Ancestral makeup, cousin matching, 3 million database, Gedcom upload, Chromosome browser, Raw DNA download, Health results are at additional cost, and Privacy concerns Yes

CHAPTER XVII

GENEALOGY RESOURCES

INDEX TO WEBSITES

One of the free genealogy resources is Familysearch.com. There you search your ancestors by name and come up with thousands of people with the same name all over the world. You must put in additional facts to help narrow down your search to get your ancestor.

This is not the only way to search on family search.com. They have historical record collections which cover places all over the world. You can find collections from pre 1700s to present day. For example they have Alabama county marriage records from 1809-1950 and 1818-1936. Let's say you are looking for Australia or South Australia, immigrant ship papers or Dominican Republic misc. records from 1921-1980 they are there. Many times you will see a small camera like object next to the entry and this will allow you to see the original document.

You can also go to one of the search libraries in your state or town. There you can search on their computer for information and they have some microfilm there and you can order any one you may need for a small fee. Once it arrives at your library you can go back and view it on one of their viewers.

The Mormon's website also allows you to add your family tree that you have started. By doing so they will send you an email if they see a connection or record that pertains to your family listed in the tree. If you go to "Memories" at the top of the page you will find pictures, gravestones and documents pertaining to your ancestor. Also clicking on "Family Tree" and then "Find" you can type in a name and it will bring up family trees with that person's name in it. The best part of this website is it's FREE.

Here are a list of websites I found to be helpful in my research. They are found throughout this book but I will list them here for easy access.

GETTING STARTED

www.biblerecords.com/surnames.html- Bible records

www.blacksheepancestors.com- Prison records

www.ancestorhunt.comprison_search.htm – Prison records

CENSUS

www.us-census.org- census

www.familysearch.org- census

www.census-online.com/links/- census

www.censusfinder.com/index.htm- census

www.censusrecords.com- census

www.powwows.com/am-i-native- American Indian

BIRTH, MARRIAGE, DEATH & DIVORSE

www.nyhealth.gov/vital_records/processingtime.htm- to order copies of BMDD

www.searchforancestors.comutility/birthday.html- calculate birth and death years

www.familysearch.org/search/collections/1202535- social security death index

www.archives.gov/atlanta/public/railroad-retirement-board-records- railroad workers

www.deathindexes.com/- death by state

www.odmp.org/search/browse- fallen police officers

www.virginiaobits.homestead.com/- Virginia census from 1790-1940

www.legacy.com- obituaries

www.findagrave.com- cemeteries, tombstones and memorials

www.wolfbane.comicd/index.html- Int'l classifications of disease/ Cause of death

www.google.com –search engine

MILITARY RECORDS

www.ancestry.com

www.familysearch.com

www.3fold.com

www.militaryindexes.com/revolutionarywar/ -Revolutionary war records

www.achives.gov/contact.inquire-form.html -form for pension records

https://aad.achives.gov/aad/index.jsp -WWII records

http://spec.lib.vt.edu/civwar/guidecw.htm -Civil War Manuscript Collection www.nps.gov/civilwar/soldiers-and-sailors-database.htm -Civil War Soldiers and Sailors records

www.genealogytoday.com/genealogy/answers/W_prisoner_inf ormation_in_particular_military_prisoners.html -Military Prisoner records (spaces are underscores)

www.digitalarchives.state.pa.us/archive.asp -Civil War Veteran Cards

www.digitalarchives.state.pa.us/archives.asp?view=ArchivesInd exes&ArchiveID=9 – Mexican Border Veteran Cards

www.digitalarchives.state.pa.us/archive.asp?view=ArchiveIndex es&ArchiveID=6 –WWI Service Metal Application Cards

www.digitalarchives.state.pa.us/archive.asp?view=ArchiveIndex es&ArchiveID=8 – Spanish American War Veteran Cards

www.digitalarchives.state.pa.us/archive.asp?view=Archiveindex es&ArchiveID=13 –Revolutionary War Military Abstract Cards

www.digitalarchives.state.pa.us/archive.asp?view=ArchiveIndex es&ArchiveID=18 – Militia Officers Cards

www.digitalarchives.state.pa.us/archive.asp?view=ArchiveIndex es&ArchiveID=21 – PA National Guard Veterans Cards

IMMIGRATION, NATURALIZATION & SHIP'S LISTS

www.gensearch.com/ports.html - List of smaller ports of arrival

www.gensearch.com/neworleans/quickguide.html - New Orleans immigration port

http://khuish.tripod.com/ships.htm - Ships and passengers lists from different countries

www.archives.gov/research/immigration/passenger-arrival.html - National Archives Website

https://aad.archives.gov/aad/series-list.jsp?cat=GP44

Immigration Passengers arrival

www.libertyellisfoundation.org – Ellis Island

http://www.theshipslist.com/1847/index.htm - Ships list 1847

http://www.immigrationships.net/ - Ships lists

National Archives, what is available

All censuses from 1790-1940

Census of Manufacturing
Pa. mortality census
Vermont Agricultural & industrial census
Virginia non- population census

Revolutionary War Records

War of 1812 Records

Mexican War

Civil War Union
Civil War Confederate

Spanish- American War (1898)

Selective Service System

World War 1
World War 11

Native American Records

Records relating to enrollment of eastern Cherokee
Correspondence of War Dept., re: Indian affairs
Enrollment 5 civilized tribes- Index to final rolls
Cherokee census roll
Old settler Cherokee settler rolls

Naturalization Federal court
Name index, Petitions, Military petitions, Declarations of
Intention & Naturalization

Passenger and immigration

ALMSHOUSE, ORPHANS, WORKHOUSE & POORHOUSE RECORDS

https://www.olivetreegenealogy.com/orphans/ - Orphanages

www.genealogytrials.com – Hospital records

https://dp.la/ - Digital Public Library of America (hospital
records and much more)

CHURCH RECORDS

http://baptisthistoryhomepage.com/ - American Baptist Historical Society

http://genealoger.com/lutheran/luth_church_records.htm - Lutheran Records (spaces are underscore)

https://www.swarthmore.edu.friends-historical-library – Quaker Genealogy

http://mcusa-archives.org/MennObits/index.html - Mennonite and Amish

http://www.newhorizonsgenealogicalservices.com/church-records.htm - Church records

CEMETERY RECORDS

www.findagrave.com – Tombstones and memorials

www.daddezio.com/cemetery/junction/CJ-PA-001.htm - Pennsylvania Cemeteries

www.ccapgh.org/cemeteries.asp - Catholic Cemetery Association

http://www.interment.net/cemetery.htm - Cemeteries around the world

HISTORICAL SOCIETIES AND LIBRARIES

http://www.acpl.lib.in.us/home/research - Allen County Public Library

www.worldcat.org? – World's largest card catalog

https://library.si.edu/ - Smithsonian Library

https://archives.org/index.php - Nonprofit library with free books

INTERNATIONAL RECORDS

https://en.wiktionary.org/wiki/Appendix:Latin_forms_of_English_given_names – Latin names with English counterparts (spaces are underscores)

www.findmypast.com – Genealogy website

http://worldgenweb.org/ - Genealogy site for the world

www.ukcensusonline.com/ - UK Census

www.nationalarchives.gov.uk/ - English records

https://www.ukbmd.org.uk/county/yorkshire/parish_records_ - Yorkshire Parish, England

www.genuki.com – Library of Genealogy

http://titheapplotmentbooks.nationalarchives.ie/search/tab/home.jsp - Tithe Applotment Ireland

www.donegalgenealogy.com – Irish Genealogy

https://registers.nli.ie/ - Catholic Parish Registers

www.donegalcoco.ie/culture/archives/digitisedarchives/ - Donegal County Council

http://discovery.nationalarchives.gov.uk/ - Irish Genealogy

www.rootsireland.ie/ - Irish Genealogy

http://www.dippam.ac.uk/ - Irish Immigration Database

www.doaghfaminevillage.com/attractions/ - Famine Village

https://www.nrscotland.gov.uk/ - National records of Scotland

www.bespokegenealogy.com/ – Scottish tax records

https://www.nrscotland.gov.uk/research/guides/census-records#open_census_records – Scotland Census

https://www.scotlandpeople.gov.uk/ - Scottish Ancestry

www.africiagenweb.com/ - African Genealogy

http://www.aa.gov.au/ - National Archives of Australia

https://www.qld.gov.au/dsiti/qsa - Queenstown National Archives Australia

http://www.arch.be/index.php?l=en&m=genealogist – Belgium/Netherlands Genealogy

http://www.french-genealogy.typepad.com/genealgie/2013/03/finding-your-franco-belgian-ancestors-just-got-easier.html - Belgium Genealogy

http://www.bac-lac.gc.ca/eng/discover/Pages/introduction.aspx - Canadian Genealogy

http://www.genealogysearch.org/canada/ - Canadian Genealogy

http://www.legacy1.net/ - Chinese Genealogy

https://cubangenclub.org/ - Cuban Genealogy Club of Miami

http://www.genealogie.cz/en/ - Czech Republic Genealogy

http://ww.ddd.dda.dk/ddd_en.htm - Danish Database

https://hisdoc.net/history/history.html - Finland Genealogy

http://afgs.org/site/ - French Genealogy

http://www.daddezio.com/grekgen.html - Greek Genealogy

http://www.dholmes.com/hafs.html - Hungarian Genealogy

https://www.jewishgen.org/Hungary/ - Jewish Hungarian Genealogy

https://www.italiangenealogy.com/ - Italian Genealogy

http://www.angelfire.com/mt/sicily1/ - Sicily Genealogy

http://forebears.io/india - India Genealogy

http://www.genealogylinks.net/newzealand/- New Zealand Genealogy

http://www.rhd.uit.no/indexeng.html - Norwegian Historical Data Center https://pgsa.org/ - Polish Genealogical Society of America

https://pgsm.org/ - Polish Genealogical Society of Michigan

http://www.lostshoebox.com/poland/online-records/ - Polish records

https://www.arkivdigital.net/swedish-genealogy - Swedish Genealogy

http://swedishgenealogyguide.com/archives/tag/swedish-birth-record - Swedish Birth Records

https://www.familysearch.org/wiki/en/Russia_Online_Genealogy_Records - Russian Records

https://tranlate.google.com – translates languages

TAX AND LAND RECORDS

Virginia research- Virginia Library
http://www.lva.virginia.gov/

Crawford County, PA
http://www.yoset.org/facilities.html#CH

Archives of Maryland-
https://msa.maryland.gov/megafile/msa/speccol/sc2900/sc2908/html/volumes.html

Virginia Tax Records
http://www.binnsgenealogy.com/

General Land Office Records

https://glorecords.blm.gov/default.aspx

Bureau of Land Management

www.glorecords.blm.gov

Google Earth to find your family home

https://www.historicaerials.com/ -

PROBATE RECORDS

Northern Ireland Genealogy including Will Calendar

www.proni.com

Website for Wills, Guardianship, Naturalization, and much more

http://www.sampubco.com

MESSAGE BOARDS AND SOCIAL MEDIA

www.ancestry.com – Message boards

www.genforum.com – Message boards

www.rootsweb.com – Message boards

www.olivetree.com – Newsletters

www.Cyndislist.com – Genealogy

www.genealogy.com – Genealogy

www.genealogynewsletter.com – Genealogy Newsletters

www.americanancestors.org – Weekly Newsletter

FAMILY & RESEARCH CHARTS

Research and Family Charts

www.midwestgenealogycenter.com

NEWSPAPERS

Google News Archives

https://news.google.com/newspapers?hl=en

Chronicling America

https://chroniclingamerica.loc.gov/

Illinois Digital Newspaper Collection

https://digital.library.edu/collections

Fulton History Old New York Newspaper

https://www.nypl.org/collections/articles-databases/fulton-history-old-new-york-state-historical-newspapers

Historical Newspapers

www.newspapers.com/papers/

Newspapers in many countries

https://www.veridiansoftware.com/elephind-com/

Trove
Library of Australia
https://trove.nla.gov.au/newspaper/?q

Penn Libraries
http://viewshare.org/views/refhelp/historical-newspapers-online-usa-2/

ICON International Coalition on Newspapers-Newspaper Digitization Project

http://icon.crl.edu/digitization.php

Wikipedia Online Newspaper

https://en.wikipedia.org/wiki/wikipedia:list_of_newspaper_archives

Genealogy Bank Newspapers

www.genealogybank.com

www.newspapers.com

Worldwide Newspaper Collection

www.news.google.com

Newspapers

www.news.google.com/newspapers

DNA

www.ancestrydna.com

www.gedmatch.dna.com

www.myheritage.com/dna

www.familytreedna.com

www.23andme.com

FOR LIFE AND DEATH ARE ONE, EVEN AS THE RIVER AND THE SEA ARE ONE

KHALIL GIBRAN

CONCLUSION

Genealogy isn't just a collection of names and dates. You are writing a story of where your family began and the path your ancestors took along the way. A world filled with suspense and intrigue.

Where did I come from? Who were my ancestors? Were they famous or infamous? Could I be related to a King or Queen? I have a history.

I have written this book to assist you in finding the answers to those questions. It is a roadmap to show you the way. Each chapter gives you tested methods in performing accurate research, along with charts and worksheets to keep all the research organized. Many websites are now at your disposal to assist you.

Knowing who you are and where you came from can open many doors. It may enhance your future. So, go forth and find your ancestors, your legacy, and your history. Learn how your ancestors lived and died. You may just be surprised when you find a little bit of yourself in each one of their stories.

So let's begin in writing your own family history story.

Happy Researching!

Janice